To. Shannon

INSPIRATIONS of

MY HEART

BY ERIN SCHENK

Erin Schenk

Erin Schenk

Higher Power Publishing
629 E. I30 Frwy Suite 208
Garland, Texas 75043

ISBN 0-9787631-1-4

First Printing Novenber 2006

Dedications

I dedicate this book to my husband, Larry, and My Dad, James Cather. "May both of them, know how much, they, mean to me".

3 **Erin Schenk**

Acknowledgements

My highest appreciation is to God for giving me the inspiration I needed for accomplishing my book. I would like to thank my husband for being a strong influence in completing my book. I would like to thank my dad for always reminding me, I can do and be anything I wanted to be. I would like to thank Steve J. King for the direction and insight that he has given me.

Introduction

In the poetics you read in this book you will see
fifteen dimensions of my True Heart; sadness, a
child full of fear, pain, criticism, strength, faith,
heartache, imagination, peace of mind, sincerity,
sensuality, passion, clarity, accomplishment, and
love. When I first started writing I was only reading
between the lines of what I was writing, until I
started reading more carefully. That is when I found
my true self in those lines and finding where I
belong. God has also been a big help. For the
wisdom He knew I had in me, that He helped me
find myself. May my words touch some part of you
that you didn't know exist, just like it did Me. Enjoy
and may we all find ourselves.

Contents

Fairy In The Mirror
My Angel's Face
Forever Friend
Each Other's Arms
Loving Husband
Take My Hand
Bring Me Up
Save Themselves
The Queen's Little Miss
Their True Romance
Reach Everything
Living With Life
Places In The Soul
Aboard This Ship
Changing Directions
Rejuvenating My Mind
Wild Spirit
Grateful For This Life
His Memory Goes On
Looking For Myself
Her Two Worlds
Down On The Farm
I'll Show You The Way
Chances
Sacred Heart
Sweet Dream Dust Fairy
Walls On Us
Bonds of Grief
Fool's Choice
Lets Go Clowning Around
Take A Look At Ourselves

A Child's Plea
I Am Charmed
Soul Searching
Peace of Mind
Want To Be
Protect Me
Demolished World
Tragedy
Don't Invade Me
Outlines In My Mind
Fortunate To Be Loved
Impressed
Dancer In Me
Tangled Imagination
Crisis
God's Ring of Hope
All I Need
Four Letter Word
The Battle Won
The Gifts
Free Spirit
Reminding Myself
Do It All
Panic
Trapped No More
Power Crush
Pleasing You
Ambers of Love
The Step Mom You Didn't Have To Be
The Love Of A King and Queen
Lord Is Welcome

Erin Schenk

Time Slipped Through My Hands
Devouring Beast
Hidden Beauty
Life Is A Gamble
Cramped Room
Brave Little Knight
Delicate Jewel
Lost Love
Soul To You
Love of Dance
Out Of This Town
Red Velvet Curtain
United Nation
Fall of Mankind
Memories Of My Daddy
The One
Don't Judge Me
Choose Your Life
Legion Of The Strong
Follow My Own
Open My Eyes
Young Lovers
Wrong For Me
I Can't, Without You
They Don't Understand
Timid Spirits
All Right, I Surrender
Honor My Heart, Hold My Hand
Still Not Rescued
To Touch Her Once
Out Of The Darkness

The Fears of Yourself

To wish for something and not knowing if it will
come true-
Lighting a candle and when you go to blow it out, it
lights back up again-
 To see in your mind the way it should be and it is
not that way-
Wondering if you'll make it through the day to see
tomorrow-
Different things seek our minds and have us
wondering-
Like wanting it to be some bad fantasy, but
realizing it is reality-
Holding true feelings inside and letting them come
out and play-
Fears of never seeing tomorrow or your future-
Making a person feel bad by what you say and not
caring if it hurts-
Listening for a answer, but only hearing a silent
whine-
Looking at yourself and wishing you, were someone
else-
You try to say something to someone, but they
don't care to hear-

Knowing the fears of unhappiness and becoming
sad-
Meaningless love you give to someone is not a true
feeling-
To chatter among friends only to put down and talk
about others-
Mouth movements, such as words, but invisibly
doing it so it won't hurt-
Crying for someone to love you, but knowing they
won't-
Changing your mind about doing something and
living to regret it-
Paying attention to a put down instead of the truth
About yourself-

Erin Schenk

Love Shows

To show someone you care is to give them love-
I'll show you I love you by giving some to you-
Once you fall in love it's hard to fall out of love-
Finding that certain kind of person to spend the rest
of your life with-
It's not always a thrill, it takes a lot of work-
Heart over matter is what they say when you are in
love-
But with you I know it is true the love that is there-
I know what love is and I know I love you-
If I never hold you again I don't want another-
Wanting you is something I need, but loving you is
something I want-
I will try to show you in every way possible how I
feel-
Only I can explain what it is that you do for me-
 I feel for you what is true and I want to be with
you-

Your Love

Shinning a light as the sun through the trees-
Beneath the night sky as we are together-
The imagination of our love is special-
Responding it there was no one around-
As you move closer I start to shake with a shiver-
Waking up in the middle of a field by your side-
Falling all around me is your sweet voice-
As I sat upon the side of your heart and wait for
you-
Come to me as the warmth and desire float-
Holding me there to you, will it never stop, as we
are here-
Beauty of love I never felt before as it fell into me-
As I am with you the feelings I hide are coming out-
The wall I built around me is being chipped away,
but not yet broken-

           Erin Schenk

Thoughts of Happiness

The countless ways we shared laughter-
And the way you pulled me through the crying and
hurt-
The joyous hours of spending time together-
The sharing of sweet secrets and wonders-
And the hopelessly silly stuff we did to each other-
The good and bad times we are there for one
another-
And all of this has been worth my wild for being
here-
The happiest of times were the best of times-
The saddest of times were the worst of times-
Here forever and always we are happy with the
sharing, caring and loving of one another-
And hoping one day we can remember-
The nights of being together on a stormy night-
And the difference you showed me in wrong and
right-
Among all these things that weren't done, we
together will be loving each other-

Dreaming of You and Me

To dream of how it should be-
To hold you oh so tight and dream of you at night-
Seeing that we are meant to be-
Wanting us to be "Always"-
Taking all we have holding on to it now-
To be together forever and always is how-
Making you smile by just being me-
Knowing we will always be-
Showing how I love you by just being there-
Sharing everything with you means how much I
care-
I have made up my mind to set my heart free-
Just remember I will be dreaming a dream of you
and me-

Erin Schenk

Trying To Hold On

Holding each other and dreaming of never letting
go-
Making love to you makes me feel wonderful
inside-
Knowing this is real or a fantasy that you only put
in my mind-
Fire burns bright and passion in our veins are the
flames-
It was a secret, but let out by one of us-
Now that I know how I want you and see it in my
dreams-
The fear of never holding you again is the way it
seems-
Lightening flashes and your face is gone from my
mind-
You are now gone, but one day you will be back-
I see a vision of you and than you are gone like a
cloud of dust-
It is hard to let you go after trying so hard to hold
on-
Nothing else matters now that you are gone-

All Alone

To walk alone and the fears of loneliness are there
inside-
Wanting something, but not really knowing what it
is-
Taking hold of that someone and wanting them to
become real-
Telling yourself the truth and someone else turns it
into a lie-
Searching for someone and no one answers when
you call-
Scared of a dream and knowing you want out-
Deep inside a dark place, a vision of a thought
haunts you-
To share my dreams with a stranger, it comes at the
worst of times, when I am sad-
The things you face in life can be scary-
Like falling in love and hoping it will last-
Looking for a future, but only seeing tomorrow-
Living without someone by your side-
Crazy things happen with your mind when you are
alone- I am scared of being alone without someone
there-
Making everything that seems lonely come to life-
Holding everything deep inside until it burst-
Never knowing why people leave and don't come
back-
Wonders seek our expectations when there is
Loneliness-

Erin Schenk

My Husband, My Forever Valentine

My husband may he always be my hero-
May he be there when I need a friend to lean on-
To you I gave a special place in my heart and there
you will stay, Forever-
"May we stay linked for a lifetime to come and to
always love each other"-
I love you from the depths of my heart and soul-
No matter what comes our way, we can make it
through it-
The bond we share is stronger than most and I am
hoping it will always grow-
Most people wait a lifetime for what we have, that
makes us the lucky ones-
I don't have to have one day out of the year to say I
love you; there are 364 other days I can say it-
My husband is my life, my heart, and the priority of
my every inspiration-
Always there to help, to be by my side and lend a
hand-
He will never let me forget how much he loves me-
I hope he never forgets how much I love him-
  "May we always be each other's Valentines"-

My Dad

You helped the seed that conceived me and set me free-
I know inside that you were there whether you were near or far- You are the reason I had so much in my life to be thankful for-
The lady that was my mother and your wife made it hard in our lives-
Because I am willing to be authentically me, is why I was meant to be-
For some reason up above I was put here for all the world to see-
Maybe at the time I was born, to show people what miracles are made of-
My Dad is the one I am proud to call my own, to be there in my heart from now on-
I know you tried so hard, but above all you are my #1 hero-
I'll never be ashamed of the man that is my Dad as long as I stand-
 I love you with all my heart from near and far-

Expanding My Time

The time on earth I spend is precious-
I can't understand why everyone and everything
rushes-
"They say, they don't have time, we all have time"-
People think life is some kind of deadline-
No one takes the time so everything will work out-
My time I am given is mine I don't want to have to
meet any deadline-
I need my time to sleep and eat, just to think-
There is time to dance and sing, there is time for
everything-
There is time for me to nourish and to even flourish-
During my time I can encourage and show my
courage-
And in this time I can cry and weep or laugh and be
happy-
I can take my time to mourn for my loses and yearn
for my wants-
With my time I can change the things I can and
except the things I can't-
With this time I can spend with the ones I love-
And even pray to God up above-
In this time I will find my place and ask for my own
space-
I'll give myself time to see things clearly-
And give myself enough time to rise early-
I'll take time to stop and smell the roses-
And walking down the path I have chosen-

I will share some of my time with charity and help
those in need-
I can't bring back the time I have lost-
But I'll try to make good with the time I have left-
I will take a minute to catch my breath-
I will make time for everything I need to do that
includes loving you-
For my time is here and now, I want you to show
me how-
The proper way I can continue growing with this
time you have given me-
I appreciate every moment I have lived and I hope I
have many more moments to live-

The Truth

To see a vision and only imagine what it, can be-
Simplifying only the truth of where it can take you-
Clarifying what you want by the touch of a hand-
Laughing like a child caring about nothing, but
love-
Smiling to hide the pain locked up inside you-
Days go by as if they're only an hour or minute-
Heartbreaks help you to grow and to keep you
strong-
Speaking to someone only in a silence you can
hear-
Shaken by a scarce feeling of loneliness everyday-
Knowing everything isn't going to fall into place-
Crying, but not knowing why it hurts so-
Running from your enemy, "yourself"-
Walking away from your fears and never looking
back-
The last word you know is the saddest, is
"goodbye"-

Be Yourself

Determining if something will come true, you have
to wish for it-
To wish upon a star and it doesn't always come true
for you-
Seek a beautiful sight you commonly see in your
mind-
Going with the bad and knowing you want to do
your best-
Whispering a secret only you and a special friend
share-
Seeing different, wonderful things deep inside your
heart-
Trying to go through life without any mistakes, but
knowing you'll run into a few-
To feel out of place and knowing you really aren't-
To practice who you really are doesn't take a lot at
all-
Be happy with what you have been given and use it
to your advantage-
People will always come and go that think they can
change you into what they want-
But the secret to this trick is to always be uniquely
you-

Wrapped Up In You

Wrapped up in you, is me, I feel the warmth of your
love-
I will always be the perfect one for you; I fit you
well-
As you touch me I melt into you-
Tangled up in the arms that hold me tight-
My heart is wrapped up in you-
Light me up with the feelings you bring out in me-
Knowing you are making me feel so right-
You take me to the highest level of ecstasy-
I close my eyes and know that I am all yours-
You bring me back to life when you kiss me there,
here and everywhere-
I am exploding inside as you take me out of this
world-
I feel so secure when I am wrapped up in you-
You take me to the edge until I can't stand it
anymore-
As you whisper you love me, it sends shivers up my
spine-
When our bodies are entwined we become one-
The cries of pleasures you bring out in me, I never
want them to end-
I hold you in my arms, my heart, and every part-
I am yours to take to this wondrous place-
As you exploded, I exploded with you-
As our hearts race from the adrenaline we feel-

Bringing each other to the highest peak and never
coming down-
We collapse into each others arms as we catch our
breath-
Now and forever I will be wrapped up in you-

Erin Schenk

Dreams

Dream mode, it is where your imagination takes
you while you sleep-
Some people may have pleasant dreams, others may
have nightmares, some may not dream at all-
Dreams can play tricks on your conscious mind and
your subconscious mind-
Don't watch a scary movie if you don't want to
have nightmares if that kind of thing bothers you-
Pleasing thoughts can lead to peaceful dreaming-
Some don't sleep because they are afraid of what
they will see if they close their eyes-
Some people talk in their sleep because the dream
they are having is so realistic-
Dreaming is not a bad thing, it is natural, so let it
take it's course-
Every creature that sleeps, dreams-
You can see in your dreams what really matters if
you just put your mind to it-
Dreams can help you determine so much if you pay
attention to them-
It is your mind trying to tell you something-
Some don't think that a dream can have a impact on
their lives, but they can have that power-
Daydreaming is normal and many people do this on
a daily bases-
There is nothing wrong with daydreaming; it just
shows you have an imagination-

Dreams can make you happy or sad, depending on
your feelings-
 Beautiful things, places and people can be seen in
your dreams-
You can use some to your advantage in making
some of your decisions-
And if you pray to God and are sincere, He will
always let you have peaceful dreams-

Erin Schenk

Danita

My sister Danita, who thinks she can do it all-
Though sometimes she may stumble and fall-
She may not be hard as steel, but in her heart she
has the will-
She has been through so much in her life, but she
tries so hard to be a good mother and wife-
She was sixteen when her life suddenly took a
change, she had to learn life from a different range-
She may also be handicap, but she doesn't take
anyone's crap-
She shows what strength is made of and knows how
to truly love- She is the one I don't get to see much,
but I hope she knows I love her and care about her
and such-
She has got what it takes to make it through all of
life's mistakes- If you could see the world she sees
through her eyes you would be amazed and
surprised-
I know sometimes when I would spend time with
her, she would be sad-
I really didn't know how to help her, that would
make me a little mad-
She is my sister this I will agree, but if anyone tries
to harm her, I will not leave them be-
I realize sometimes we aren't that close, she is one
God gave to me, the one He chose-
In some aspects I could not have her strength, at
some point I would bend and break-

With her two kids that put her through hell, in the
end it all turned out well-
And for her husband, Gil, my hats off to you for
loving her and being there, to see her through-
The day her kids were swept away from her, she
fought back with anger and pride-
"Who could blame her for that anger and pain"-
But, I am proud she is my sister and of course I will
claim her- Though Danita and I am one of a kind
and know the other don't mind-
I am glad we are sisters through this life time-
I am thankful for the love and appreciation of my
sister, how could this be any sweeter-

Erin Schenk

Love What Matters Most

You must love what matters to you the most-
The gifts that you are given from up above-
Cherish the love you share with that special
someone-
Be grateful for the friends you have-
If you just believe, love will see you through-
Whether you realize it or not, love matters to you-
Love the people that are part of your life-
Love the blessings you have been given-
Be grateful for the love you have been given to
share-
Love your spouse, your children and yourself-
Bringing with this love is a happiness that will
forever live in you-
Look around you and see the things you love and
that do matter-
Never abandon who you love and what matters to
you most-
Face that part in your heart that knows you can
love-
Just to give and receive love, that should always be
the greatest feeling for all to share-

Lace Your Heart With Grace

Decorate your heart with ribbons and lace and see
what it can entrance-
Open your heart to the adventure it has been ready
to take-
The warmth it can bring you when the lace is
entwined with your heart-
You can see through this lace but it will hold strong
to whatever you face-
The grace you feel in your heart can be tied with
this lace-
Bring this lace with you to make yourself something
beautiful-
Grace and peace is brought on by the mysteries of
yourself that you have achieved-
Embrace this ladder of self-peace you have built for
yourself-
 Create with this grace the feelings that you treasure
most-
Many things can be made from yourself grace-
To be the decorator of your heart and paying
attention to every part-
The lace you use is bright and shows your
individual self-
To your heart you give the gift of love to yourself
and everyone else-

Erin Schenk

Don't Change Me

Don't change me into someone you don't want-
Don't treat me like some wild animal you want to
run down or hunt-
I am not a wet lump of clay you can form into your
own shape-
If this is the way it is going to be, then I must
escape-
Don't try to change me into the person you think I
should be-
For when I was born that meant I was free to just be
me-
When I cry, don't tell me to stop-
If I want I will cry my every last drop-
And if sometimes I want to act like a child, just be
glad and smile-
 You will see I am only this way once in awhile-
Don't change me into not showing my feelings or
that I am afraid-
 Don't come in raining on my happy parade-
For I am me, because that that is the way I was
designed-
When God made me, He thought it out and took His
time-
I am made into what and who I am suppose to be-
So for goodness sakes don't try to change me-
I have my own special ways I do my own thing-
And as for me I don't want to change anything-

My habits are mine and if you don't approve that is
fine-
I have my own way of thinking and explaining-
The way I express myself shouldn't make you feel
any different-
And don't try to change me because you think I am
ignorant-
My mind and body is like yours, it has it's own
structures-
It would cramp your style if I tried to change you
into a hopeless rupture-
So stop trying to change me and let me be me-
Then you will see how much happier we can be-

Erin Schenk

Midnight

Midnight is when the creatures of the night come
out and prowl-
You can here the coyote's cries and howls and
sometimes even hear an owl-
When the bats come out and play and the cats go
stray-
And from evening until dawn the crickets play their
song-
As the coyotes howl at the moon-
They know morning will come soon-
For midnight is when most of the world sleeps-
Except for the creatures that creeps-
And if you are in the woods at night-
You might get a terrible fright-
Watch out, some creatures could be hiding in the
shadows-
Or lurking along the meadows-
At midnight some animals might go crazy-
And others may seem quite lazy-
Midnight is when some of the world awakens-
While other parts become quite shaken-
Some stay up all night long and hope to see the
dawn-
And other things are frightened if it happens to
thunder or lightning-
Midnight can be scary-
When things start go hairy-
Be careful not to fall-

For the creatures can see it all-
For midnight is when some animals go for a hunt-
Hoping to catch a runt-
Midnight is when you think that everything sleeps-
But for some things that is when they eat-
Waiting and watching for something to pounce-
And then devouring every ounce-
And the mountain lion's heart is pounding from the thrill-
Because it is out for the kill-
Other animals can't afford to sleep; they have to get busy in building their nests-
Though they are perfect prey for the rest-
These animals of the night have learned to protect themselves-
From us and everything else-

Erin Schenk

We All Have Wings

We all have wings, spread them out and lets go
flying-
Go as high as your heart desires, soar-
Look how high you are, feel that freedom-
Be like a bird and conquer the skies-
Close your eyes, can you see yourself flying, up, up
and away-
Angels have the wings to fly all around, up and
down-
We can pretend we are angels and fly to our
destination-
Seek that inner peace you could feel if you could
fly-
Fly high above the trees until you reach the skies-
Look you can touch the clouds, aren't they soft-
You are safe in this fantasy flight-
Reach up and embrace that light that waits for you-
You are your own angel, with the wings to go
anywhere, so fly-
See where you can take yourself to the highest
Peaks of your imagination-
Not having a care in the world when you are flying-
Open your eyes and see what awaits ahead-

In your fantasy, take that special someone with you-
Teach them to fly as free as a bird-
Watch how you both soar with grace and beauty-
If you can see this in your mind, then let it take you
there-
Don't be scared of the wings you have been given,
use them to take you on your journey-

Erin Schenk

Look Beyond The Face

No one looks beyond the face of most, they judge
the cover before they open up and take a look
inside-
They read between the lines of the person they are
addressing-
No one gets to know a person before they make
calculations that are false-
Someone who doesn't have it all is pushed aside by
the people who do-
God protects these people that gets pushed aside-
He sees the depths of everyone's heart and He
sometimes cries-
The cruelty some get because of what they don't
have-
If you don't have a certain look, than you must have
nothing-
What a horrible way to look at life-
Some have a disfigurement of some kind and the
world looks at them as if they are beast-
What is wrong with this world, we are all made the
way we are meant to be-
Take a look at yourself and think about what God
has given you- He made you exactly the way He
wanted you to look-
Take into consideration He did the same for
everyone else-
Be happy with what you see and be proud of who
you are-

He didn't make anyone the same, though some may
Look alike-
We are our own individuals, that is what makes us
Whole-
And He will never make a mistake as long as we
Exist-

Hold Me Tonight

Hold me tonight in your arms and dance with me in
the living room-
Pretend we are newlyweds, the happy bride and
groom-
Hold me tight and let me know you need me
tonight-
If I fall, you can save me and be my knight-
I am your forever girl-
So take me for a whirl-
Slow dance with me because I want to be close to
you-
I know that you love me and I hope you know I love
you, too-
 Hold me tonight, I want to show how much I care-
With you I have my love and so much more to
share-
Show me your level of tenderness-
And blow me sweet kisses-
I am waiting for you with my arms open wide-
I love you so much, it is hard to hide-
Turn back the covers-
I'll show that there could never be another-
Not so long ago we were closer than any other-
Hold me tonight and take me on a fantasy flight-
I will be that sweet and tender heart that knows your
every part-
Bring yourself over here-
I want to feel your touch and hold you near-

Kiss me until I am breathless and I am hopeless-
Hold me tonight because I can't sleep and I am
restless-
I want to feel your breath on my neck and I will
love you until you feel you are going to break-
I am yours to love for always and that is no
mistake-
We can make each other feel alive again, by doing
what ever it takes-
I want to hold you tonight-
I can make you feel so good that your heart will feel
so light-
Light me up so I can burn bright and lose control-
You will have a hard time trying to take hold-
Come closer to me I want to feel your heart beat-
My love I feel for you will sweep you off your feet-
So baby that me in your arms and hold me tonight-

Erin Schenk

Blind Love

Blind love cannot see, it can only feel-
It knows when this feeling is real-
It doesn't ask questions or look for answers-
But it does know how to nurture and pamper-
Blind love cannot be taught-
Or even for that fact be bought-
It won't runaway or hide-
This love will always be on your side-
This love doesn't know the meaning of "no"-
Onward and upward it will grow-
It doesn't show shame-
Or look to blame-
It can feel your pain-
And when you are feeling strain-
It will give you a reason to stay-
This love will never stop or delay-
It will find you and take hold-
It shows its colors so beautiful and bold-
This love is easily spread-
It will never bring you dread-
It will also do it's best to perform-
In you it will be your new form-
This love won't leave you behind-
If you look close it easy to find-
It will show it cares-
It knows how to share-
It will not bring you down-

With this love you won't wear frown-
It has a special personality-
Has no technicalities-
It will help you get along-
This love will show you were you belong-
It is something you can't learn from a book-
It has no certain look-
Blind love can last forever-
It will leave you, never-
It doesn't care if you act like a fool-
It will put you on it's pedestal-
This love is not sorry-
Will bring you no worry-
But blind love glows so bright-
That it can make you feel so right-
Love is God's precious gift-
The one He is always willing to give-
He gave His only son to show His love-
There is no other like Him that will ever rise above-

Hide and Seek, The Cat

Shh! Be quiet can you hear that-
It sounds like it is coming from under that hat-
What can it be, a bird or rabbit-
Oh no, I think it is that crazy cat-
"Why would that cat be under there"-
To make us think he isn't here-
For he is an old crazy cat-
Thinking we would not find him under that hat-
He likes to play hide and seek-
Because he is a little sneak-
He hides wherever he can-
In the hamper or behind the broom and dustpan-
Sometimes he will hide in the trees-
Or maybe in a pile of leaves-
Wherever he can find a spot-
Sometimes he'll hide in mom's flowerpots-
He likes to hide in my closet-
But me sister's room is where he leaves his
deposits-
On her bed he leaves her presents-
Like mice and birds and even their scent-
He'll hide behind the couch waiting to run out and
pounce-
He is steady and fast, never misses a bounce-
He likes to hide under the skirted end table-
Where he is waiting ready, willing and able-

He has habit of being a pest-
To get our attention he makes a mess-
He is too busy to sleep-
So I don't know where he gets his energy to jump
and leap-
He'll follow me outside because under the toolbox
in dad's truck is his favorite place to hide-
The flies, he loves to swat at and as we watch, mom
says, "that crazy cat"-
But above all Hide and Seek is quite a cat-
Especially when he tries to run into the house and
runs into the patio door with a "smack"-

Childhood

Childhood is the time to just be a kid-
And try not to do what your parents, did-
This is when you think you want to grow up so fast
And at the same time have a blast-
It is when you have your favorite coloring books,
games and other cool toys-
It is the time for tea parties and Barbie dolls-
And all the other dolls that are big and small-
When you have your favorite little racecars
And you pretend to be some famous sports star-
When it was okay to have ice cream all over your
face-
And you wanted to enter a kiddy car race-
When you laugh and giggle under the covers
And you must mind your mother-
It is the time when there is no other greater man
then your dad-
Though sometimes you make him mad-
It's when you wake up everyone early on Christmas
morning so you can see what Santa brought you-
And no matter what you get into your parents still
love you-
It's when daddies will play Shuttes and Ladders-
And you try to be good so you don't make your
mom any madder-
Sometimes you can be a brat and sometimes you
like to aggravate the cat-

Sometimes you think you are a great baseball star
with your plastic ball and bat-
Having fun jumping on the trampoline-
Or pretending to be ballerina queen-
It is when you play cowboys and Indians
And with your little train engines-
Making crayon marks on the wall
And knowing sometimes you are just to small-
You like playing at the park-
And sleep with a nightlight because you are scared
of the dark-
You have your favorite cartoons
And you wish you could go to the moon-
You don't want to get up and go the school
Or when your mom kisses you in front of your
friends, that just not cool-
It's when you think your older brother or sister is a
weirdo
And they think you are just a kiddo-
Going to grandma's house was so much fun-
Because she would let you have cookies, cakes and
cinnamon buns-
You were excited about the new bike you gotten-
And knew grandpa would spoil you rotten-
When you liked eating hotdogs
And catching big slimy frogs-
You would bring your mom a bouquet of weeds and
she would say "how sweet"-

And when it was gross for girls to play with boys
and boys to play with girls-
When you would climb trees because you wanted to
be like the squirrels-
Sneaking cookies and snacks into bed
And having your favorite book you read-
Little girls playing dress up in their mama's clothes-
And little boys spraying the dog with the water
hose-
It's when you are the apple of your mama's eye-
And daddy's little spy-
When a kiss made a boo, boo feel better
And your mom reminds you to put on your sweater-
When you liked playing in the snow no matter how
cold-
"And you would go around saying, I never want to
get old"-
One minute you are pouting and mad-
The next you are happy and glad-
Your experiment with eating play-do-
And realizing you rather eat cookie dough-
You are taught it is not nice to stare
And you never want to comb your hair-
You had a hiding place for that stash of candy-
Where you knew it would be handy-
And you wanted a puppy so bad-
But when it chewed off the head of your Barbie or
Ken or G.I. Joe man, it made you so mad-

Having a contest with your best friend to see who
could scream the loudest and then sharing a big
bowl of ice cream-
Making bubbles with your bubble wand
And going pollywog fishing at a near by pond-
This is just a reminder to all you kids big and small,
that childhood will always be around-
So play until your heart is content or until you fall
on the ground-

Erin Schenk

Crying For the Heart

Cry, cry, cry you broken heart let it out-
Don't be selfish with your feelings, share-
We all hold too much in that small space we call
our hearts-
Break this torture you put yourself through-
Crying because of past pains will not change a
thing-
Where will it take you except to a sad link-
Heal your heart by being connected to a strong
bond-
Deepen that strength you know you have-
That crying will only keep you down-
Oh, my we don't want to do that know do we-
Crying for the simple fact that you know you can-
After awhile that is no way to get the attention you
want-
Be brave and be bold, be you and don't cry about
being you-
You are you for the same reason everyone else is
their selves-

Lines

Lines, they are all around, up and down, in and out-
In the stores at the registers, as people wait-
Lines can determine between two points, yours and
mine-
Watch there is lines in all we do-
Lines appear anywhere, from here to there-
On the map or on your lap-
Draw a line and open your imagination, look at
what you can create-
Beauty can be brought out by lines-
Lines connect the dots and a whole lot of spots-
There are lines you can follow to get to where your
heart can take you-
Follow these straight lines you have made and don't
worry if you stumble a little along the way-
The lines will always keep you on the right track-

Beauty Within

Your beauty comes from within-
There is no need to pretend-
Awaken that inner beauty that lives in you-
And she can be soothing-
Bring back your self-affection-
And then take a look at your reflection-
There will be something different you will see-
And say to yourself, "this is me"-
You call on someone else to help you look
beautiful-
But it has to be you that feels beautiful-
You put yourself through so much abuse-
But in the end what is the use-
There is a beauty in all of us-
Take sometime to make a fuse-
Don't put yourself down-
And stop wearing a frown-
If you look deep enough you will find her-
She is there-
She is not in what you can buy-
But she can be shy-
So let her out-
And see what comes about-
In each one of us there is a goddess-
And our bodies are her office-
So hire her, she can make you feel proud and sure-
This beauty, let it come out today-
Believe me you will want her to stay-

Whether you are skinny, chunky, tall or small-
There is one in us all-
She can creep up on you out of the blue-
You never knew she was there, you never had a
clue-
You are the one that holds her back-
And puts her in a paper sack-
She is the beauty you read about-
That makes you want to pout-
She doesn't measure your amounts-
She can help with what counts-
She is there when you sleep-
And knows you have no need to weep-
She will make you feel so alive-
Give you a reason to thrive-
She wants to show she cares-
So treat her fare-
She will take her responsibility-
And show you your possibility-
She'll remind you she just wants some of your time-
She knows you should have nothing to hide-
So let her come out and watch her bloom-
If you give her a chance, she will cause you no
doom-

Erin Schenk

The Sweet Sound of Rain

Listen, listen you hear the rain as it hits the roof-
Falling from the sky is God's sweet tears of heaven-
Go dancing in the rain as if you don't have a care in
the world-
We sleep like babies when it rains, listening to the
sound-
Let the rain fall down on me and see me sing and
dance all around-
Run through the puddles it may leave, don't worry
you won't sink-
The rain is something we all need, let it be-
The flowers and trees will get all they need-
Rains come today and leave some other day-
We all need the rain to flourish and grow, I want
you to stay-
But not so much we flood and wash away-
The rain is the perfect cure for dry land-
And mixes so perfect with sand-
Rain just always be around, landing on the ground-
You are the most precious gift from up above-
Just know that you will always be loved-
You can run fast or slow, you just go with your own
flow-
Filling up the lakes, oceans, rivers, ponds and
streams-
What a hard time keeping up, at least that is the way
it seems-

Bringing down with you from the sky the thunder
and lightning-
Bangs and booms is the sounds we hear playing
along with you-
And if you have your way you will always be
around, to fall down-

Erin Schenk

Natures Wonders

There are so many wonderful natural things all
around us-
Why don't you just take a look at theses wonders-
The way the rivers flow to the seas and know where
to exactly go-
The birds knowing when the seasons are changing
and when it is time for them to go south-
The winter's snow coming just at the right time,
knowing it is the time to fall-
The animals scurrying to gather their food for the
long winter rest-
The bears and their habit of taking their long naps-
Spring with its rains, thunderstorms and tornados it
may bring-
As the flowers and trees sprout with new life-
The temperatures start to rise and here comes
summer-
And it is all amazing how everything works
together in nature to keep the world going around-
The stars in the sky all having a story of their own-
The sun and the moon, they know when to rise and
fall, above all-

Safe Place

A safe place is where your heart is happy and
warm-
A place to lay your head for the long night's rest-
A place you call your own little nest-
This place keeps you from the rain and snow-
It is a place you already know-
It surrounds you in the comforts you need-
Where you always take your lead-
It's a place to lay your hat-
And also there you can take a nap-
A place where you can be a cook-
Or a place you can read a book-
It's a place where you can plant flowers-
Or take a nice, long hot shower-
A place to get away from the outside clatter-
And all the distracting and useless chatter-
A place you can laugh and play-
And a place you know you will always stay-
A place where you can be alone-
Or talk for hours on the phone-
A place you can untangle your mind-
Or a place to just unwind-
In this place you can never go wrong-
And a place you can stay up all night long-
This place you know by heart-
Here in the place you play your part-
In this place it is familiar to roam-
It is the place you call home-

Erin Schenk

I, Am Not You

You laugh at me, but you are then one that looks
stupid-
To let you know you are not cupid-
You think you got it all-
Because you shop at the mall-
You make fun of me-
But you are the one that is funny-
You think you really are something because you
have money-
But Honey, you really are nothing-
You pretend to have pride-
But there is something you hide-
You show your temperament-
And say things you never meant-
You deprive yourself of time-
And keep running in overdrive-
You blink once, you blink twice, third time there
goes your life-
 Slow yourself down and take a minute to put your
feet back on the ground-
When you are rushed, you scream, yell and cuss,
that is just nuts-
You wonder why people look at you and say to
themselves, "I, am glad I am not you"-
You wear all the latest styles-
If I where you I'd burn them in a pile-

You think everything has to be perfect from your
head to your feet and everything in between-
It just rattles me; you think you are some beauty
Queen-
 If we were all perfect then the world would be
quite a bore-
And there would be no need for an uproar-
You like all the new movies and think they are
groovy-
Not me, I stick with the oldies, the one's with
meaning-
You shame the people with the way they do there
own thing-
And you put them down because they don't have
the most expensive things-
You are your own destruction-
Don't bring on that self eruption-
Play your cards right and give yourself one more
chance to shine-
Don't take offense to what I say, I am just getting
some things off my mind-
I have nothing against anything or anyone; it is just
so many don't pay attention-
To let you know you have to love yourself before
you can love anyone else, if this is something I
forgot to mention-

Butterflies

Butterflies flying all around me, I watch them
dance-
They are saying, "come on and take a chance"-
They wonder around to flower after flower, minute
after minute, hour after hour-
They are free, like the birds and bees-
With their beautiful colors, they can blend with the
flowers-
You can see them in your dreams; they're graceful
as can be-
They are part of God's beautiful creations-
Butterflies are big and small-
You can't count them all-
I watch them fly-
 And wish I could fly-
As they land on my shoulder-
They couldn't be any bolder-
They are a natural wonder-
Like the rain and thunder-
Butterflies are going to fly all around-
They bring with them the peace that everyone
needs-
Catch them in a net, and then let them go and watch
how free they are set out to be-
They are red, orange, yellow and blue, all the colors
that are so true-
Caterpillars in their cocoons-
They are getting ready to bloom-

They come with a new and beautiful life-
Butterflies come fly with me-
You were meant to be-

The Sweet Smell of Flowers

The flowers have many sweet scents, just take a
smell-
The flowers know the seasons so well-
Flowers well grow with the special care you give
them-
They are saying, "watch me bloom"-
I will grow in your gardens or in your flowerbeds,
just plant me-
I will have many blooms, I will have plenty-
Be like the flowers, grow and see what you can
become-
With proper care you can be that beautiful-
No flower is the same, just as you and I-
With love you can change a dying flower, like you
can change-
You must find the flower that best suits you, from
the color to the texture-
Plant the seeds in your heart and watch the form
you will take-
The right one for you will never be a mistake-
You can have the same sweet smell of the flower
that was made just for you-
Believe in this trilogy of the flower to turn you into
what you want to become-

Sweet Command

Soak me up in the lavishes of your love-
I will fit you quite well, just like a glove-
I can make your every fantasy come true-
I will cling to you and stick like glue-
My lips are sweet like good wine-
And my arms will wrap around you like a vine-
My body will cause your rapture-
As for your heart I will capture-
Your every wish is my command-
Give me time, you will understand-
I will catch you in my forbidden web of passion-
I will do everything that you had only imagined-
I can break that cycle that was undeniable-
For everything I do, I'll hold you liable-
Your knees will feel so incredibly weak-
You will not even be able to speak-
With my love you will learn-
With it the more you will yearn-
I will have you climbing the walls-
I will be there when duty calls-
I will be something that you cannot break-
Give you all the love you can make-
I am that shiver that runs up your spine-
With what I do to you it will make you feel so fine-
For I am that taste that will last-
I will make you so thirsty, you will drink me up so
fast-
With all my simple pleasures-

Erin Schenk

They will be ones you can't measure-
No need to sweat it and worry-
I am in no big hurry-
But for you I am starving-
I'll take my time to satisfy my craving-
Just run your fingers through my hair-
I promise I'll be fare-
I will do it all with my style-
You give me an inch; I'll give you a mile-
I will give you all I have got-
My voice and touch will leave you dripping wet and
hot-
I will leave you feeling so jaded-
You know when you feel it, my love has not faded-

His Strength

Help me to be strong and even when I am wrong-
Help me find my way and please listen when I pray-
Help me to know what is right and thank you for
my sleep at night-
Help me to reach to up above and thank you for the
man I love-
Help me achieve my goals and when things start to
unfold-
Help me to look beyond the face and to find my
special place-
Help me to just hold on and to understand I will go
on-
Help me to never be sick and to know your love
runs thick-
Help me find what I have been looking for and to
know I can be much more-
Help me realize you are really there and thank you
for the care you share-
Help me to pull myself together and to go on
forever-
Help me not to fall and to know I can conquer all-
Help me to believe in me and to see the things I
need to see-
Help me to understand and never say, "I can't"-
Help me when life can be cruel and not to look like
a fool-
Help me when I am in denial and feel I am on trial-

Help me be creative and to understand I am my own
native-
Help me get through my crunches and to roll with
the punches-
Help me live while I am alive and not to get so far
down that I want to cry-
Help me rid the demons that maybe in my head and
break their invisible thread-
Help me with my personal movement and to live
the best of every moment-
Help me find my spotlight and let it be the one that
is right-
Help me with things that maybe incapable and to be
steady and able-
Help me with the ability to love myself and with the
ability to be one's self-
Help me realize my mistakes and there are others I
know I will make-
Help me with things I can't resist and let me know
you exist-
Help me not to be left behind and to use all of my
mind-
Help me with the questions I may ask and to
accomplish all my tasks-
Help me to keep my focus and know that I am not
hopeless-
Help me, Oh, God to fight the odds and so much
more-

Your Individualism

Individualism, makes you who you are-
We all have are own individual star-
Don't run in that tunnel that will turn you bad-
Turn your world away to the things that make you
sad-
Be your own positive triangle-
Take it to your own angle-
We are given the choice-
To raise our voice-
Don't look for someone else's imprint-
Make your own print-
We are all given something different, our own
selves-
Our personality cannot be the same as anyone else-
We all have our own way we learn
And the way we yearn-
Stop the wishing I was someone else syndrome, all
you face is doom-
Don't hide yourself in some far away room-
It doesn't make you any smarter playing someone
else's part-
 Bringing yourself down because someone is
putting you down, that is their own work of art-
To think you aren't any good because someone else
doesn't think so, that is their own opinion-
Just remember their own individual candle is
burning at both ends-
 Sooner or later they are going to burn out-

Erin Schenk

So take a chance to turn yourself into something
that they thought you would never be-
And say, "I live my life because it is mine, if you
Don't like that, it is fine"-
Feel all right with who you individually are and set
out to make your own star-

In My Head

There you are in my head again, get out of here-
You, are not welcome to enter my mind, you bad
thoughts-
Don't try to hold me back when I try to run from
you-
You are the thoughts of my past-
I am going to hit you with a blast-
You think you can control who you think I need to
be-
Get out of my head and set me free-
You cause confusion of my emotions and bring on
the pain-
You bad thoughts like to see me cry like rain-
I am not going to let you get me today-
I will put up my guard and fight you off everyday-
You think you can rattle me-
But I will win the battle you give me-
You hide in the greaves of my mind and wait to see
if you can bring me down-
I will flood you with good thoughts and cause you
to drown-
I am going to get my way-
You are not welcome to stay-
Stop playing around in my head and causing
trapping webs-
I want you to be gone; there is no room for you
here-

Erin Schenk

Secret Weapon

My secret weapon is one you will never guess-
It is one you never thought I posed-
And, no it is not the breast upon my chest-
It is not something you buy from the store-
It can't be bought and it so valuable and so much
more-
You can't see it by just looking at me-
You will never guess what it can be-
It is something I can't live without-
But it may want to scream and shout-
You have to look into me so much deeper-
Just to let you know it is a keeper-
It is something I show, if you just take a look-
Before you know it, it will have you hooked-
It is something that will never hurt-
Though it can be a flirt-
It can be quite stimulating-
It even gives with no refusing-
I can't give this to anyone else-
It is mine, it is my inner self-
It treats me good, even when I fail-
And it knows when I am not well-
It runs strong through me-
It gives me everything I need-
When I need it, it is always there-
I know it is not going anywhere-
It is the window for my heart-

It will never tear me apart-
It brings me peace and serenity-
And it lets me know I have it's security-
We share a bond that will never be broken-
Though we really never have spoken-
It will never let me forget who I am-
And helps me find what I am looking for-
It knows me better then anyone-
And knows exactly who I should become-
It will never turn it's back on me-
It will let me dance, laugh and be happy

Erin Schenk

Leave Me Your Heart

Leave me with the heart that I love and I know
loves me-
With this heart I can always find the peace it brings-
Don't let this heart that loves you ever go-
My heart and soul will go with your flow-
What my heart feels for you, makes me fall in love
with you all over again-
I know one day we will both be gone-
But today lets share the love our hearts bonded-
Our hearts run to each other with strong emotions-
So leave me your heart with all your true notions-
My heart will be the one that loves you the most-
I am glad your heart is the one I chose-
To you I will give my heart-
And love you with every part-
Turn our hearts into love's true water fountain-
Together with our hearts we can conquer
mountains-
We will find a way to always share them-
Leaving each other that special place in our hearts-

I'll Give You Everything You Need

I'll give you my love, my life, my heart and my soul
until we grow old-
From here to there I will be everything you need
and last for a lifetime-
I will give you the moon and stars; the key to my
heart-
We can make a brand new start to give each other
everything we need-
My tender arms will hold you forever and to be
strong enough to catch when you fall-
I will give you the attention that I would not share
with another-
I can show you I will bring you brighter days than
any other-
I will be the warmth you need when you are cold-
Never think that your life is empty as long as I am
near-
I will hold you high on my special love scale-
I will give you the love that I have made for you-
The light that is burning in my soul is just for you-
I will take my chances to love you every moment, I
love you so-
And when I am feeling weak I know you will be my
strength-
I hold strong to your heart, the one that can give me
everything I need-

Erin Schenk

An Old Indian Story

I am an old Indian, with a tale, the one I love so
well-
As we sit around the campfire tonight this is the one
I will tell-
"There once was a young warrior so brave and
sure-
And things to him looked obscure-
With me, I had other brave warriors along for the
ride-
With my horse and I painted up, we're ready for
battle-
My warriors and I rode bareback; there was no need
for a saddle-
As we ride through the woods with our bows and
arrows-
Together we conquered the enemy, there was many-
We will kill them swiftly and fast-
They will know they have been hit with a blast-
My horse, he was steady and strong-
He could run for however long-
For however long it may take-
We will win, that is no mistake-
We will hunt you down until you all lay on the
ground-
Through the air our arrows were flying all around-
We scalped them with our tomahawks and left them
for dead-
I know with my aim I'll hit my target for sure-

They wanted to fight and now we won the war-
We won that battle with true defeat-
And they ran and hid and tried to retreat-
There was never any question of our glorious
mission-
 "But there would never be another battle like that-
He would say, "We won that victory with pride and
glory"-
As he gets older and we get older, we will never get
tired of his stories-

Erin Schenk

Old West

The old west when times were rougher-
And you had to work a lot tougher-
Cattle ranchers with their ranches-
They had to take their chances-
Where cowboys camped out under the stars-
 And Indians with their painted arts-
When family meant something-
And everyone had nothing-
When you would sleep from dusk until dawn-
So you could work hard all day long-
 People appreciated what they had
And didn't run around mad-
When you were happy to help your neighbor-
So both could make good on the fruits of your
labor-
The cowboys in the saloons-
With all it's regular tycoons-
When times were less crazy-
And people were less lazy-
 Families would bow their heads in prayer-
And showed God how much they cared-
Where you drew your water from a well-
 And it was time to eat when you heard the dinner
bell-
When sitting on the front porch was quiet and
relaxing-
As you watched your children dancing and playing-
And now the Old West, its times are at rest-

Absolute Silence

Absolute silence is all you can hear-
Your heart is racing from the fear-
Then you hear a shrilling noise-
You have nowhere to run, you have no choice-
But inside your head you can hear that voice-
 Saying run, run as fast as you possibly can-
I am here, I am the boggy man-
I come into your dreams while you sleep-
And I can run through you deep-
The silence you hear is me in the back of your
mind-
The door you slammed in my face is the one I'll be
waiting behind-
I live in your head, not under your bed-
You can never rid me, I will never be dead-
You think if you hide under the covers, I will go
away-
I am not in your closet, that is not where I stay-
I stay where you can always see me-
I am everywhere, so where can I be-
There is never a way you will know where I am
about-
But when I jump out at you, you will shout-
I will file myself into a secret slot-
I will be hiding, but you won't know what spot-
I can cram myself into your shoes-
And knowing your balance you will lose-

Erin Schenk

I can hide anywhere I please-
I will not burn or freeze-
I could be in that clock on the wall-
Or in that tree that stands tall-
But remember I live in your head-
That is where I cause the most dread-

Outside My Front Door

Outside my front door is the whole world to
explore-
I don't know if there is much I want to see
anymore-
 And plus I have no idea what I would be looking
for-
I know in my heart this world is falling apart-
Life outside is just pushed along like a shopping
cart-
Everything moves so fast-
That nothing last-
As the world may crumble around me-
I am scared of what may come to be-
A lot of people look for life's answers in a bottle-
While some never find what they always been
looking for-
I know some lay curled up, crying wanting more-
There is no point in doing those things to myself-
The world inside my life is not one I would display
on a shelf-
Though my world is probably better than others-
Some adults still see the world through a child's
eyes-
There are children that have to mature faster just to
survive-
And others get no discipline when they do wrong-
The world plays one of the saddest songs-
There are people who will kill just to get a meal-

Erin Schenk

While some have the ability to heal-
And there are people who go through life, living
through hell-
And other people that are always sick and never
well-
There are people who go through life waiting for
the should bee's-
Instead of excepting the could bee's-
Some just go through this world looking for a fight-
While others wonder where they are going to sleep
tonight-
The world is slowly and continuously going down
hill-
Some people get by with what they can steal-
The sad part is this world is not the one God made-
Man made this world what it is today-
We blame Him, but we did it to ourselves-

Train of Thought

My train of thought it can't be bought-
Though sometimes it's all I got-
I know if I don't use it, it just might rot-
It helps me keep myself on track-
And helps me rewind my mind and play it back-
At times it reminds me how to act-
And also helps me face the fact-
Some thoughts I may abuse-
And others I will just refuse-
At times some may bring me madness-
While others may bring me sadness-
Some thoughts of my past I would rather do
without-
And others just want to make me shout-
There are many that would make you cry-
While others would make you feel you want to die-
The thoughts of the slaps across the face-
And the thoughts of the name-calling and feelings
of disgrace-
There are some thoughts I wish I could erase-
Some get my mind going at a faster pace-
The earlier thoughts of happiness are few and far
between-
While some I use as a mental lean-
Some make me feel so depressed-
And I know I have some I'd like to express-
I have some that sometimes drives me wild-
And those that make me glad I am not a child-

Erin Schenk

I have so many, I wouldn't know where to start-
They all play a significant part-
Every thought I have is every part of me-
If I just pay attention to them, I can see what I need
to see-
There is some I need to keep to myself-
While others I put back on my mind's shelf-
I know some can be pleasing-
And others can be quite disturbing-
There are some I need to control-
And others I should never let take hold-

Courage, Curiosity and Chaos

Listen; listen to your courage it is trying to tell you
something, be brave-
Your curiosity is taking hold; look at what it has
found-
The chaos of your busy life-
"Whoa" slow down is your courage in check-
That little thing called your curiosity would like to
know-
Take a minute and check before the chaos sets in-
Our courage can make us strong if we just use it-
The curiosity we feel would be much smoother-
And the chaos would be lighter-
To have courage to stand up for yourself and others,
is a noble trait-
Your curiosity can help you learn and expand your
mind-
The chaos you may get into sometimes maybe
confusing-
If you have the courage to face the chaos head on it
won't seem so hard-
Our minds are constantly filled with curiosity, so
explore it-
Use the wisdom you are given to determine between
the three-
You will be surprised of the way you look at them-

Erin Schenk

Courage is something that everyone has, but it is
Your choice to seek it-
Your curiosity is waiting for you, find what you are
looking for-
The chaos is getting in your way; clean it up and all
will fall into place-

"Oops" I Did It Again

Oops, I did it again opened my mouth at the wrong
time-
Bad habit, it is always getting me in trouble-
"The I did again syndrome", some people have it
and some people don't-
It is a shame because sometimes it gets in the way-
Realize it and fix it, you can do it with a little
practice-
Pay attention to your instincts when you know it is
about to happen-
Keep your mouth shut and your thoughts to
yourself-
Bad habits are hard to break, for instance, talking
about someone, keep quiet-
Don't say anything at all if you can't say something
nice-
Behave yourself and watch how things will change-
You open your mouth and speak your mind at some
of the wrong times, be quiet and listen-
Don't interrupt, that is just rude, listen to what is
being said-
Don't try to put your two cents in if it's not going to
matter-
Watch out for this syndrome and learn from it-
In the long run it will pay off-

Erin Schenk

Illusions

Illusions can be given or they can be taken-
Some will make you feel numb and some will make
you feel shaken-
They play with your mind and cause you to lose
control-
They can make you feel like you are falling in a
hole-
Watch out, they can make you feel lost-
Are you willing to pay the cost-
They may send you to a magical place or they will
send you to a far off, dark place-
They will change their pace if you give them the
space-
Some can have you feeling wonderful-
Others can leave you feeling doubtful-
They will be there even if you aren't aware-
Understand they will always be near-
Some can be very limiting-
And others can leave you screaming-
There are ones to make you lose your ability-
And some can help you face reality-
They can cause you to go crazy-
Then there are some that are totally amazing-
They will sometimes make you feel you are in a
endless game-
They may make you feel you are in a pool of
shame-
They can cause such confusion-

Be careful of the one you have chosen-
That illusion maybe your explosion-

Erin Schenk

Brightness and Darkness

Brightness, is what you see when you open your
eyes for the first time-
This is a better place then in the darkness-
Darkness can cause you conformation with your
inner being-
Brightness will bring with it peace your soul has
been searching for-
Darkness will take you to places you never wanted
to see-
Believe in the brightness to take you to a higher
self-
Be aware of the darkness, it will play tricks on your
mind-
The brightness will keep you from these tricks-
Brightness is where you can take your stand-
Darkness will be that place your sadness will land-
The brightness will always be there to remind you,
to smile-
But the darkness will try to take over again, defeat
it-
Brightness is in the face of a happy soul-
Darkness is in the face of a sad soul-
Let God help take you to this brightness He offers-
Don't let the devil take you to his darkness-
From the brightness God gives you it will help you
see the goodness in your soul-

Be willing to take the brightness that God has
offered and open your heart-
And see what comes about-

Erin Schenk

Open the Doors

Behind door number one, there you are, take a good
look-
Happy with what you see-
You think you can do it all, wrong-
Be careful, don't over indulge yourself-
Behind door number two, is where you think you
want to be-
Look around, is it a safe place for your heart-
Watch out, it could be deceiving, listen too-
Behind door number three, what is this, surprise-
Just what you have been looking for, "happiness"-
So put that smile back on your face you haven't
seen in a while-
Feel better now, you found what you were looking
for, your well-being-
Always be happy with the door you have chosen-

Pain

Pain can run through you deep-
There can be pain when you sleep-
It can hurt you so bad-
Especially when you're depressed and sad-
When it is caused from depression it's a continuous
ache-
There is pain when your heart breaks-
There is pain when you are done wrong-
Sometimes it hurts so bad, how do you go on-
Pain can be caused mental, not just physical-
It wraps itself around you and it can be brutal-
If you let it, it can have a chain reaction-
It can bring you down to its level of action-
It will cause you to cry-
And beg, steal and lie-
 It will devour you and eat you alive-
It diminishes what makes you thrive-
Certain words can cause pain-
It will run right through your veins-
This world is full of so much pain-
It can cause you to go insane-
There are so many different kinds-
It will sometimes just tear up your mind-
It has the power to change the way you feel-
Some can be so hard to heal-
It can cause you to crumble inside-

Erin Schenk

While at the same time send you on a downhill
slide-
It can cause you to have a hard time getting up
again-
Sometimes you think, "when will it end"-
It's stubborn and sticks right to you and wants to
stay-
You can't get rid of it; it doesn't want to go away-
Like a sharp knife it keeps cutting away, at you-
It just keeps cutting deeper, so what's the use-
You have to fight and break free-
Break that cycle of misery-

The Voice

I woke up in this deep, dark space-
I just wondered to myself, "what is this place"-
It was somewhere I couldn't explain-
I just thought, "am I going insane"-
It felt like a place I 'd been before-
I couldn't get the feel of it, I wasn't for sure-
I heard this voice calling my name-
The voice was familiar, but sounded full of shame-
Then it started having this raspy tone-
It became louder like it was speaking through a
microphone-
Through my head these pictures ran-
Could it be someone I know, maybe a friend-
Than I heard this scream that would shatter your
bones-
And then there was shrilling and screeching tones-
By now my head was pounding and my heart was
racing-
What is happening to me, am I hearing things-
The voice sounded as if it was getting closer-
It said, "you are the one I have chosen"-
And then it said, "I speak to the unspoken"-
I live in this dark, secluded, far off land-
I am not human, nor even a man-

And it said, "just give me time and you will
understand"-
As we spoke, it said, "I am here to help"-
But I could not see, was it here to help-
I couldn't tell where it was coming from-
I felt it was all around me, echoing-
Repeating these words, "continue running"-
For I couldn't get what it was saying, I didn't
understand-
I just thought, "is this some sick joke"-
Then I heard the screaming again- I asked the voice,
" what am I running from, a friend"-
"No!" it said, "just run until you get to the end"-
Again I asked, "what am I running from"-
Then the voice replied, "a man in a mask"- It just
kept repeating, "keep running"-
For this man is not someone, but something-
I didn't have a clue of where to go-
It was dark, how was I suppose to know-
There was this noise that came from behind-
It said, "you are going to be surprised at what you
will find"-
I heard this screaming over and over-
The voice said, "just keep coming closer"-
The man in the mask was hiding in the shadows-
Waiting and wondering if I was going to be scared-
There was this loud, cracking sound-

Like someone was banging on the wall, "pound,
pound, pound"-
The voice I was hearing suddenly disappeared-
And the man in the mask appeared-
He was tall and dressed in black-
He said, "that voice you heard is not coming back"-
Now I felt trapped and unsure-
Suddenly I became dizzy and everything became a
blur-
The man said, " don't be scared , I am not here to
hurt you"-
I will protect you from the voice that wants you-
For the voice is the one wearing the real mask-
I am just doing my job like I was asked-
Now I was confused at what to do-
Then I woke up and realized it was just a dream-

Erin Schenk

My Anger

You sometimes seep into my dreams at night-
For you are some unknown sight-
As you were barreling through my mind-
I tried to screen you out time after time-
It's like you can't be scared-
You would say, "there is to much we shared"-
And you would say, "I keep you on track"-
Now on me you have turned your back-
And I would say, "I never wanted you anyways"-
You thought I wanted you and asked for my praise-
I knew you were something I could do without-
For you were the reason I fused, fought and
shouted-
You would pound in me, your music-
I guess you thought I could use it-
You are the anger that use to burn inside me-
But I found a way to set myself free-
You are the anger I never wanted to keep-
You played with my conscience and caused me to
lose sleep-
As I use to run around angry and mad-
I have found no reason to, now that I am glad-
From now on you are not going to get the best of
me, you just won't-
For I am not going to let things bother me like you
did-

You use to dance around with the dark clouds in my
Head-
But now these clouds are gone-
And as for us, we are done-
No more coming in when ever you feel like it-
For I must learn to control you and fight it-
You caused so many people to be angry at me-
You were my problem; you were the key-
You would come in and unlock me when ever you
Wanted-
 I don't want to wear your token of anger around my
 neck-
You can go unload on someone else's deck-
Good-bye anger, for your ship has left-

Fairy In The Mirror

Who's face in the mirror do I see, is that me-
I am as happy and free as I could be-
With my bow and arrow, I go through the meadows
to and fro-
Bringing with me the happiness in the mirror this
morning I had seen-
With this smile on my face-
I'll make this a happy place-
I'll play you a happy song on my lyre-
And those tears will disappear-
I am that fairy in the mirror, who's never looked
more sweeter-
Lets go to greener pastures to see all we can
capture-
From the birds and bees and the flowers and tress,
lets go see all we can see-
We'll fly all around from the sky to the ground-
I'll cradle you in fun-
And we'll dance in the sun-
When I am your fairy-
I'll help you with the burdens you may carry-
I'll sprinkle you with my magic dust-
And make your sweet dreams my must-
I am that fairy in the fairytales you love so well-
I fly like the breeze as I move through the trees-
Your days with me will be brighter-

As I can make your sadness lighter-
In this world we have a lot to explore-
And together will see much more-
With you, I will share my love and my care-
Just remember if you need me I will always be
there in your dreams-
I will give you praise and walk with you in grace-

Erin Schenk

My Angel's Face

My angel's face is one that you cannot en-trace-
She watches over me as I move through my days
with ease-
She is the one I do not see-
She keeps me from falling down-
And looking like a clumsy clown-
I know she is always around-
Because in the background I hear her sounds-
She is there with a hand on my shoulder-
I will still need her, as I get older-
She knows when I am low-
And goes with my flow-
She knows if I am angry-
And sometimes I go a little crazy-
And when I am happy, I know she is glad-
Because I am not sad-
I know she floats by when she hears me cry-
She knows all my feelings and will let them pass
by-
For my angel's face is the one I would like to trace-

Forever Friend

From afar I could see this guest-
He carried my hopes in a chest-
He gives me the hours to complete my needs-
For His wisdom He feeds-
His life He gives to everyone-
But He has a hard time getting through to some-
He watches every little thing we do-
And crumbles to pieces everything that is cruel-
He sees when someone is being trampled upon-
And He knows how long He'll let us go on-
He has the highest of any authority-
He is the ruler over every majority-
For we should listen when He speaks-
He is the one who can push us off our peaks-
He is a good listener, but it's His choice to answer-
He can strike anyone He pleases with illness or
cancer-
I just hope when I die I go to His place-
He has given me so many chances and gone with
my pace-
He knows I will ask when I need Him most-
I can't help to feel sometimes lost-
He gives me what was meant for me-
And I know He will help me be all I can be-
He can help accomplish everything that needs to be
done-

Erin Schenk

For He has no need to run-
He knows when everyone's times should come to
an end-
If you ask the Lord, He will be your forever friend-

Each Other's Arms

She could hear the sound of the falling rain-
He whispered gently out her name-
It was cold outside and they were going nowhere-
He kept her warm by just holding her near-
As they cuddled by the fire-
Their passion was filling up their desire-
He was the light in her eyes-
All he wanted to hear was her passionate cries-
As the night began to grow long-
They both knew with each other they couldn't go
wrong-
For his heart she knows is where she will always
be-
As he reaches out and touches her, she was all he
could see-
She melts from his breathless kiss-
She thinks to herself, "I am in heavenly bliss"-
As there passion for each other grows strong-
They know in each other's arms is where they
belong-
She is the appetizer he hungers for-
From him she is craving more-
They know each other's needs so well-
That pleasing one another can never fail-

Erin Schenk

As the sighs of pleasure come from both their
mouths-
For they horizontally dance to the rain so well
needed from the drought-
As the fire slowly dwindles away-
In each other's arms is where they will always stay-

Loving Husband

There was pounding and banging coming from
outside-
It kept getting louder and closer and the motion was
rapid-
She went outside to take a look-
But nothing was there, only a hook-
She went back in and laid back in bed-
There it was again, this time it sounded like it was
hitting lead-
She got up again to go see, when she got to the door
it stopped-
As she was going back to the bedroom, it started
pounding on the rooftop-
She heard a knock at her bedroom window-
She could hear the wind blowing through the
willow-
She couldn't figure out what was going on-
There was something very strange going on-
She went to the phone to call the police, but it was
dead-
Now she was scared as frightening pictures ran
through her head-
 Her husband was gone on a business trip-
She had no idea sometimes his mind would slip-
She knew that there was something not right with
him for awhile-
There was these strange calls she was getting that
sounded like a child-

Then the lights in the house went off-
She thought she heard someone outside cough-
She panicked and went to make sure the doors were
locked-
Then at the front door she heard a knock-
The door slowly came open; there was a figure in a
long coat-
She was scared, she recognized the coat-
It was her husband, the one playing with her mind-
She thought to herself, "what happen to my loving
husband that was so kind"-
A neighbor called the police and said they heard a
terrifying scream come from next door-
In the house her husband wrestled her face down on
the floor-
 When the police arrived they found her dead-
The only evidence they could find was the plastic
bag on her head-
For they know it was her husband, but he already
fled-
They had seen this before, to the last woman he
wed-

Take My Hand

Take my hand to a far away land-
We won't care if it rains, we can pretend we are
planes-
As my inner child wants to come out to scream and
shout-
It can be your chance for a life long romance-
If you take my hand, I can show I understand-
I will help you wash away your fears, dry your
tears-
I will treat you so good, you will feel the way you
should-
So stop that crying, start that smiling-
If you are strong you can get through with what is
wrong-
Just take my hand, I will always be your friend-

Erin Schenk

Bring Me Up

Bring out the sun to dry up my pain-
I want to stop coming down like rain-
I want the things in my life to stop going insane-
I will run with my arms open to you if you will just
bring me up-
I am putting myself in your hands the man I trust-
Bring me up however, you must-
God, I see your bright star from afar-
When I see it I know that is where you are-
I kindle my time for I want to get this life right-
So please answer my prayers tonight-
Lift me up, for I want out of theses ruts-
Especially before I lose my mind and go nuts-
Lord, I would like to inherit some of your
knowledge-
So with your strong hand pull me out of this wedge-

Save Themselves

I may need help with the bridges I may cross-
And with the salvation when I feel lost-
For my enemies will try to bring me down-
They are the one's inside wearing a frown-
One person can cause the most damage among
themselves-
They are not happy unless they are bringing down
everyone else-
 Some look for any trouble they can cause-
Never caring what they do, they do it just because-
They rip someone to pieces, just so they feel peace-
That is sad they hurt someone else for anger they
release-
Not caring about the consequences when they do-
They are just miserable and they want everyone else
to feel that way too-
They see no way to bring themselves out of their
hole-
So to cause trouble that is how they feel whole-
I pray for those people who do these, things-
For they are the ones that bring themselves shame-
Always looking for someone else to blame-
I know there are things I shouldn't have done-
But for some it is a continuous thing they do for
fun-

Erin Schenk

I know there will be other bridges I will have to
burn-
But I know there will be some that will never learn-
All I can do is watch out and save myself-
And hope that others can save themselves-

The Queen's Little Miss

Among all the women I wear the crown-
I am the one in the pearl white gown-
I have hair of shinning red-
With it placed elegantly atop my head-
And curls are wrapped around my face-
My gown is covered in lace-
My shoes are satin white-
And my corset is way to tight-
 But I know I have to look my best-
For I am here to please all the rest-
Everyone I am delighted to see-
They know I am their precious Queen-
I am the ruler since the King died-
I stayed strong, they never knew I cried-
I have been alone for two years-
Though I have shed many tears-
But I am happy for it's an engagement ball-
My daughter is marrying the man she loves most of
all-
For I am proud she has found happiness-
But she will always be my little miss-
Her father would be proud if he were here-
Because to him she was always his little dear-
She will be marrying soon, in late June-
Hoping she is as happy as the king and I-
She was the most precious thing in his eyes-

Erin Schenk

And hoping she knows she will always be
"My Little Miss"-

Their True Romance

He stood there and watched her dance-
She sent him a noticing glance-
From the first time he saw her, he was taken by her
beauty-
She thought he was an adorable doll and quite a
cutie-
The next song he asked her to dance-
She accepted, as she took a chance-
Nobody had any idea this was a true romance-
People didn't know they were husband and wife-
They just pretended this was the first time they met
in this life-
They danced together to almost every song-
For they knew they would be as one a whole life
long-
They would sometimes act like this to keep things
alive-
Their true romance is one they that put forth the
effort to make it thrive-
From the first time they kissed, they knew they
would be together forever-
Each time their eyes meet, he knows he doesn't
want another lover-
He is the true crowned king of her dreams-
And every time he touches her, she melts like ice
cream-

It would suit them just fine if they were the only
two in the world-
Everyday they are thankful for being brought
Together by the Lord-

Reach Everything

Saying everything I need to hear-
Draw me close, draw me near-
The chambers in my heart play their own song-
I seek something great, for harmony I long-
The stringed instruments serenade my mind-
For the words I hear must be kind-
For my shelter is not to be disturbed-
From my window I watch and observe-
I shallow out my pool of thoughts-
And things you say can't be bought-
The answer I wait for, there is not one-
Seeking a spiritual past, but there is none-
Now cradled in absences I do not feel-
Plundering forward like a non-stop wheel-
Threading you and your words together-
 Believing that nothing can go on forever-
You crawl to a destination I can't see-
To break it all to change directions and flee-
You stand close, but I cannot reach you-
I felt everything inside reach out to you-
I dream I am in the closes aspect of your touch-
Here I am wanting and needing so much-
My confusion is nowhere to be found, gone-
I know I have reached everything, home-

Living With Life

Life that is something you have to live with day in
and day out-
Face it, it is here to stay and it is not going
anywhere-
What can you get out of life, "peace, love and
harmony"-
I did finally, you would be amazed what I have
discovered, "my true self"-
Look in the deepest part of you and see if you can
find a life worth living with-
You can if you look deep enough, search hard; your
almost there-
 Life is not all that bad if you know how to embrace
it-
Keep a promise to yourself to live your life to the
fullest-
Search for that person you were made to be in this
life-
Be happy with the outcome, because that is who
you are, don't change a thing-
Just do things for yourself and others to make your
life a little less complicated-
Become something thought you could never
become-
Life will always work its way around you, but you
must take that life that satisfies you-

God had our lives planned out for us, so take His
Advice and seek that life that is waiting for you-
Life is sometimes hard to face when there is
conflict, so just keep your head up and hit it head
on-

Erin Schenk

Places In The Soul

Your soul, has it found what it has been looking for-
Are you surprised at what you have found-
The warmest feelings we have exist in our souls-
Souls make us complete with who we are-
Everyone has his or her own individual soul, no one
is the same-
Isn't it wild that we all have our own souls-
The souls of the dead never die; they are always
floating around-
Your soul can help you choose between right and
wrong-
A good soul will be a Great Spirit one day-
A bad soul will float around lost, forever-
Your soul can go up or down when you die, be on
the right path so it can rise up-
The soul can help you believe in yourself, just listen
to what it is saying-
Be bold, I am here to stand behind you every step of
your journey-
I keep a watch out for the blows that may come
your way, pay attention to me-
If you can see the strength in your soul, you will be
able to conquer your world-
Search hard there is a good one deep inside
everyone of us-

Aboard This Ship

This ship that sails among the seas-
Is full of happiness and glee-
Aboard this ship is nothing sad-
This ship has fairytale creatures that are glad-
They laugh and play all through the day-
But at night the fairies fly away-
To spread sweet dreams to every child-
While the princes threat the princesses gentle and
Mild-
On this ship all your dreams come true-
Because aboard is one happy crew-
For the pirates on this ship are nice-
You can dance around with the mice-
They send their happiness to all the children-
On this ship there are a endless supply of treats-
While aboard this ship you aren't scared, but brave-
For the pirates and crew will sail you around the
World-
And as for this fantasy you will forever hold-
Little elves keep your dreams locked up in special
Trunks-
For this ship will never be sunk-
In the depths of your mind is this ship-
So go for an adventurous trip-

Erin Schenk

Changing Directions

People continuously change directions never
knowing where to go-
Randomly shuffling with every flow-
They never settle for what they have, always
wanting more-
Their direction is weakening even if they haven't
been that way before-
They wear themselves out always going the same
Direction-
Moving forward they have lost their connection-
It's not fare they don't find the right way-
They get lost and that is how they stay-
They walk around in a tunnel vision-
Never being able to make there own decisions-
Their self-direction has been confused-
Corruption in what they feel, abandoned and used-
I want to go in my own direction, for it's better-
I will not climb a non-existing ladder-
I will settle for the direction I am head in-
For some don't they know what direction to begin-
Some change their direction for the better, some for
the worst-
They may never change to a different course-
Always wondering why they were left behind-
Others knowing they never can make up their mind-
Slow and steady will keep you in right direction-
And help you with everything in life that needs your
Attention-

Rejuvenating My Mind

Breathe in and now out, relax your mind-
It is your personal tool, so be kind-
Erase everything that has maddened your day-
Let your body relax, listen to soft music as it plays-
Cleanse yourself of your daily mess-
While relieving your hectic stress-
Your mind is your strongest asset, so give it a rest-
It is what helps you perform and do your best-
Treat it as if it is your most prized possession-
Your mind must recharge so it can pay attention-
Read a book, give it a workout-
If you just use it, it will help you know what
everything is about-
It needs constant practice and reminding-
You may have to play things over, keep rewinding-
A mind is a terrible thing to waste-
For it has it's own acquired taste-
So use all you have got-
As soon as you realize all it can do, you may not
want it to stop-

Wild Spirit

I am a wild spirit, you cannot tame me-
Like wild horses I want to run free-
I climb the mountains and their highest peaks, so
Please just let me be-
You think you can capture a spirit so free, but all
you are doing is crushing my dreams-
I roam through the countryside to the rivers and
Streams-
My wild spirit is the only one I see-
As I run with the horses-
We take our own course-
The spirit I carry is so rare, like a wild colt or mare-
As I sit on top of my mountain, into the sunset I
stare-
It is up to me in this place what I think or care-
I am that wild spirit you hear about-
One you can't hold, you have to let shout-
I am my own natural medicine that will never run
Out-
The wild spirit that lives in me will always be there-
I am that spirit that moves everywhere-
Can the spirit that lives in you, bring you here-
You wild spirits come run with me and see how
much we share-

Grateful For This Life

Thank you for this life you have given to me-
Grateful to you for you have opened my eyes, I
have more to see-
And the patience you have given me so I can find
myself-
I am grateful for it all, for life itself-
I have opened my horizons to new paths-
Ones that I hope will not pass-
I thank you for the air I breathe-
And grateful for the ground I walk on beneath-
Bring me the grace I need so I will not break-
And harmony to see me through the mistakes I
make-
Thank you for the people who have came and gone
in my life-
And letting me grow and become a wife-
Grateful for helping me realize you will always be
there for me-
 And also for helping be strong, when I really
wanted to cry-
Gracious for the food I may receive-
And not letting me be the one to deceive-
Thank you for everything and much more-
And thank you for just being there, Lord-

His Memory Goes On

A shadow appeared on the wall, but there was no
One there-
As she was reading over play she heard a voice
Speak to her-
"Come With me, I have so much to share," but
When she looked there was no one there-
She thought to herself, "maybe I am working to
Much, I am tired and such"-
Then the shadow moved across the room-
Coming back out of the kitchen dancing with a
Broom-
Pretending to dance with the broom like a happy
Bride and groom-
The shadow comes to visit every night-
And wants to hold her tight-
It was her conscience telling her to let herself go-
To let her hair down and dance with him slow,
Because he loved her so-
He was a spirit lost, but found by her-
Because in his past they were together before-
She thought she was dreaming of her husband that
past away many years ago-
She just never could let his memory go-
He knew if he did this and convinced her, she could
Move on-

Her heart was happy once again, for the love of her
Life was at home-
While back in her heart that felt empty-
For when they were together, she had plenty-
He wanted to make it clear it was okay for her to let
him go-
For he didn't want her to hold her life back for him
anymore-
She knew he could not want anything more than
happiness for her-
The emptiness she felt is forever no more-

Erin Schenk

Looking For Myself

I don't care what you say-
My love will always stay-
You are my life, my love, my heart, you are where I
started-
While looking for myself that is when I found you-
I need not look any further for what I had been
looking for-
Finding traces of what to become came from your
love-
I found I need not hide myself any longer-
My heart is now stronger-
Looking for myself I found the true me-
The one that was hiding inside me-
I look to you for some support-
And I found my heart's escort-
I never found myself until I found you-
Because of you, I shine true-
Not scared of what I might have to overcome-
Just knowing I am loved-
Looking for myself I see a lot I didn't want to
become-
I guess what I found is that I am the lucky one-
My heart jumps for joy-
This maybe the life I can enjoy-
For you are really a special friend-
I know you will see me through to the end-

So many are scared of you-
But you only do things to get your point through-
You can be everyone's friend if only that they give
you a chance-
Maybe even help someone else find themselves'-
God, I just wanted to thank you for helping me find
you and myself-

Erin Schenk

Her Two Worlds

There is this little girl who switches back and forth-
She claims it is cool for all it is worth-
From her reality world to her fantasy world-
She says in her reality world there is too much
realization-
But in her fantasy world it is as all beyond her
wildest imagination-
Her realistic world is to complicated and harsh-
In her fantasy world the weather is always like
March-
In her real world her parents are unhappy-
In her fantasy world they never seemed so happy-
In her real world there is nothing but them fighting
and pain-
But in her fantasy world they are loving and she
doesn't cry like the rain-
The real world she lives in, she feels abandon and
lost-
The fantasy she dreams of is her parents won't
abandon her at any cost-
She feels her parents are falling out of love-
In both her worlds she wants most is happiness
above all-
All she ever wanted was that both worlds to come
together-

And her fantasy world would make everything
Better-
She loves both her parents so very much-
So doesn't understand why they want to hurt each
other and such-
 Maybe her parents will realize they are tearing her
little world apart-
And realize she loves them with all her heart-

Erin Schenk

Down On The Farm

Down on the farm there are cows that moo-
While the rooster crows, cock-a-doodle-do-
There is fat, muddy pigs-
And goats that eat branches and twigs-
In the barn is where the cats hang out-
While the horses in the coral run about-
There is a big red tractor beside the barn-
So much work to do down on the farm-
The cows have to be milked-
The garden needs to be picked-
All the animals have to be fed-
The cats in the hay is where they make their bed-
They hear the dinner bell and know it is time to eat-
But be careful you might get trampled by their feet-
And the farmer knows it is also time for him to eat-
Then off to bed for everyone to sleep-
For tomorrow it all has to be a repeat-
In the morning you hear the rooster crowing-
And you know you better get moving-
While you work hard all day long to make good on
the fruits of your labor-
Sitting on the porch sipping lemonade with your
family-
These are the memories you will savor-

I'll Show You The Way

Come with me I'll show you the way to what you
have been looking for-
If you just follow me I can give you so much more-
With my way all you have to do is just ask and
pray-
Watch the things that seemed impossible, become
possible-
Just ask for my help I will show you the way-
You may not see it at first, but if you are patient it
will work-
I am the one you call to, I live up above and I am
the one you can love-
I can be the one to bring joy and misery to your life-
But in the end I'll make everything alright-
I help you carry the burdens you carry-
And the worries you worry-
When I hear you cry-
Believe it or not, I know why-
I know what you are feeling-
And thinking and when to start the healing-
If you are sincere when you ask, I will be sincere
when I answer-
I will show you the many different ways life can be
better-
Open your heart to me and I will make things less
bitter-

My way will show you that patience will endure
Forever-

Chances

Chances, life throws them at us everyday-
They sometimes cause you to have to pray-
I had some chances I have taken-
And some I have mistaken-
You have to take chances to make things right-
And hold that someone you love oh, so tight-
Give yourself the chance to learn to dance-
And to give the one that hurt your feelings another
chance-
Don't go hiding, show who you really can be-
I take mine by just being me-
You can take a chance at romance-
And show your true colors and prance-
Don't limit your chances of being happy-
If you ask me, that is just plain crazy-
Chances are, if you don't take them you'll never get
far-
Take a chance and see if you can seek who you are-
But the conclusion of this is, "you'll never know
who you can be or where you can go if you don't
take chances"-

Erin Schenk

Sacred Heart

A sacred heart is an amazing work of art-
It can contain the love that grows-
This love in your heart, you can expose-
Claiming its stake for mending, the other hearts that
break-
It is strong and knows it must go on-
Its creativity can show how to love and nurture-
With this love it has a reason to go further-
Solidly designed with each one of us in mind-
Its strength can be built and from within, can be
kind-
It can take you as far as you need to go-
You will know when to slow yourself down and
take a rest-
And give you what you need, for you to do your
best-
With it's motions-
Your heart can help to control those painful
emotions-

Sweet Dream Fairy Dust

Quietly I stir about not waking anyone in the house-
Tiptoeing around the beds quiet as a mouse-
Sprinkling my sweet dream fairy dust upon their
heads-
For the children are pleasantly sleeping in their
beds-
No bad dreams will come upon them tonight-
For I'll protect them with all my might-
They are snuggled down all in their beds fast
asleep-
For their slumber is peaceful and deep-
My job is to keep the bad dreams away-
 Give them dreams where they can laugh and play-
Take them to sweet and serene fairylands-
Or to a place that is sweet like, Candy land-
Every child can be as happy as they're suppose to
be-
Traveling to a wonderful world of make believe-
Where all their sweetest dreams come true-
There is no need for sadness or feeling blue-
You can pretend to be anything you want to be-
I am the fairy that makes many rounds all around
the world, every night-
To make sure all the children are snuggled and
tucked in tight-

Erin Schenk

Walls On Us

A long walk to approaching death-
It is that walk between birth and death-
There will be moments you never want to forget-
And others that are hard to forget-
The exhibits of silence and dread-
That feeling of no emotion or compassion, it just
feels dead-
For I can't imagine the things to come-
But for what has happened, I'd like to forget some-
The world is slowly falling apart-
No one really loves with all his or her heart-
The walls of the world are coming down on us-
Slowly diminished with every passing day-
Some people have forgotten what it is like to pray-
We have been given so many chances to keep these
walls strong-
But it seems all we can do is continue doing things
wrong-
Blaming someone else for our own actions we have
caused-
Just keep tearing them down without any pause-
Chipping away the foundation that makes us whole-
One day the wall will come down with a loud,
trembling roll-

We will shake and shimmer in ways we never
thought of before-
 For then we will not be, anymore-
We will come to an end before we know it-
For God will know for sure, that we couldn't hold
on to it-

Bonds of Grief

Grief and death is what it takes to bring the bond of
a family together again-
So many think it is where life ends, but in reality
one begins-
Bonds of grief shouldn't be the only time a family
looks to each other-
Death shouldn't be the only time when you think
you need one another-
Everyone needs each other at all times-
Like God, He is there when we need Him most-
A family shouldn't be each other's ghost-
When death comes around that is the only time the
bond is strong-
When family is that far apart, life feels wrong-
More than death should bring a family together-
Love, compassion, strength, and life should hold a
family forever-
Being close is more important then anything else in
the world-
No money or material things can pay the happiness
of what a true bond will hold-
No matter how far you are this bond shouldn't ever
be broken-
A family is God's most priceless and precious
token-

Remember the one's that love you most are the
one's you never paid attention to-
Pay attention to your family and a whole different
kind of bond will grow-
Give love and you will receive love in return and
you will realize how lucky you are-

Erin Schenk

Fool's Choice

Pay attention you babbling fool-
Being an idiot doesn't make you look cool-
You run off at the mouth-
And you go north when you should of went south-
As many times you have been to my house-
You still pass by like a speeding mouse-
You don't listen to my instructions-
Your hard headiness will be your destruction-
You think you know it all-
But in the end you are the one to take the fall-
You try to cram everything into so many days-
Hoping to get extra praise-
Saying the wrong thing at the wrong time-
Can causes my attitude toward you to be sour as a
lime-
You drive me crazy-
Because sometimes you can be so lazy-
Don't be left behind-
I know you can use your mind-
You raise your voice-
To let me know you have a choice-
Don't put yourself down-
And act like a foolish clown-
Put a bright smile on your face-
And win your personal race-
You indulge yourself in pity-

Thinking you are the one that shouldn't feel guilty-
Don't hang yourself with a thin thread-
Be proud and left your head-
If you lose your inner peace-
You will lose your self release-
So don't be a fool-
Yourself respect, is the secret tool-
If you can't see, look closer-
And realize you are not a loser-
Fools can't look at themselves because they are
afraid they have failed-
But you can look at yourself because you haven't
failed-

Lets Go Clowning Around

Come on lets go; I want to have some fun-
So I can pull myself out of this slump-
We can play at the park-
Hide and seek in the dark-
I want to forget my troubles-
And just go roll and tumble-
Or play in the sand-
And take a walk hand and hand-
Go make funny faces at the people in the store
windows-
Take me, come on I want to laugh and play-
We can pretend we are kids again and act like we
did back then-
You can push me on the merry-go-round until I feel
like I am going to fall on the ground-
Lets chase each other through the backyard-
And I can pretend to put up my guard-
I want to act like a little girl again-
And you can be my secret little boyfriend-
We can run a race down the street-
I promise I won't cheat-
It may sound a little crazy-
But Baby, come on amaze me-

Take A Look At Ourselves

We don't look at ourselves with our own eyes-
Or figure out why we want to sit and cry-
We hide ourselves deep and far-
So we really don't know who we are-
We are so far under pressure-
That it is hard to measure-
With that hole in your head-
All you face is dread-
Patch yourself up with your strive-
 And use you mind in full drive-
The voice you heard, told you that looking at
yourself is good-
The higher we go the more we are understood-
Look at all we can create if we just find ourselves-
That is what makes us human beings, is being our
self-
We are given our lives to see if we can find our own
side-
It takes a lot of energy of searching on life's long
ride-
We give ourselves symbols and signs that no one
else understands-
We all have our own interests and skills and what it
takes to show our will-
No one is responsible for you but yourself-

Erin Schenk

When you find that marvelous person and realize it is
that hidden part of yourself-

The Heart He Broke

As she cries into her pillow-
The wind blows through the willow-
Her heart is broken-
For the love he has stolen-
She once thought their love was pure-
But now she isn't sure-
She looks for the one who tore her apart-
Hoping they can make a new start-
He once carried her away in his arms-
And promised her no harm-
She is confused-
Because she feels she has been used-
He said he would never lie-
And he would never make he cry-
He promised he would always he there and show he
cared-
She had no idea he'd break her heart-
And leave her there to fall apart-
She is miserable and shattered-
Her feelings have been battered-
She wants to know why he said goodbye-
She knows he won't call-
And she don't know if that would help at all-
She wonders what she did to make him leave-
His being gone, she just couldn't believe-
She looks at herself in the mirror-

Erin Schenk

Hoping to see things clearer-
With him gone, she thinks to herself, "how will I go
on"-
He was her knight in shinning armor-
She thought he would never hurt her-
As the months past she realized he was not coming
back-
So she put his memories in a big sack-
She, told herself there will be another-
And she did find another-
It has been many years since this happened-
And she is happily married to a man from
Manhattan-
One that she knows will always stay-

The Light

This radiant light comes upon the land-
It made the rocks turn to sand-
Moving rapidly across the way-
And the waters washed away all the decay-
The birds flew towards this light and knew it was
magic-
It was a light that no one had ever seen before-
Warm and beautiful surrounding everything and so
much more-
It held it's own amazing and invigorating glow-
Everything in this light was in motion of moving
slow-
The plants and trees moved with this light-
There has never been a light like this come into
anyone's sight-
So bright and bold, but not blinding-
It's like it could be touch without burning-
Soft and gentle like the clouds up above-
For some reason it felt as if it was filled with God's
love-
You could see it from hundreds of miles away-
As it came closer, you felt your sorrow go further
away-
Shine, shine of wisdom, love, peace and glory-
For this light that shines has such a deep story-

Erin Schenk

"Follow me" that light is saying and see what
treasures I hold-
So sacred of anything that has ever been told-
This light can be brought into your world-
There is no need for rancor-
This light extols a more illuminating metaphor-
Finding this light is the first step to the rest of your
life-

My Grandmother

As she entered the room every head turned-
Her beauty was so breath taking, the people could
only wonder-
She had an exquisite way of moving across the
room-
She was like the most unique flower to ever bloom-
The smile on her face was only one she could
claim-
She had the happiest soul that could brighten any
day-
She lit up the room like the sun's rays-
But when she talked that was another story-
And the way she could make everyone laugh at the
smallest jokes-
Her backward way of calling everyone by the
wrong name-
But we all knew whom she was talking about-
Her splendor was that she loved all-
If you need cheering up she was the one to call-
You never seen someone with such joy in their
heart-
The love she gave was her own work of art-
She knew how to make everything alright-
She could make everyone's day sunny and bright-
With her wacky cake and the times she could be
silly-

You couldn't help but to love her, simply-
She never had the disposition to envy others-
She is a woman I'll always love, she was my
grandmother-
As she would play the piano and sing to me-
I would think to myself, "how lucky could I be"-
That I had a grandmother so precious and sweet-
She never had one bone in her body that could be
cruel or mean- She was a mystery and romance kind
of woman-
But Papa was her true romance-
And he will always stand by her and be her man-
To others she was Grandma, but in my heart she
will always be, Meme-

My Grandfather

He was called Papa by everyone-
He usually rose with the sun-
His temper was one I didn't care to see-
But as long as you didn't make him mad he was
sweet, as could be-
He was the light in Meme's eyes-
He thought it was cute how old movies made her
cry-
He was a housepainter in his younger years-
And I never saw him shed a tear-
He would spend time with me in the porch swing-
When I was young he was my everything-
He would play Barbie's with me but told me not to
tell anyone-
I would sit in his lap a lot while he would watch
C.N.N-
His favorite thing to do was fall asleep in his chair-
He would watch Meme's soap operas with her,
tolerated my cartoons-
But his favorite thing to watch was old westerns-
I hope he knows how much I still miss him-
In my heart he will always be a rare gem-
Papa was the serious type, but loved Meme with all
his heart-
And with him I always tried to be good, but he
knew I was a little sweet tart-

Papa will always have a special place inside me
where he will stay-
And I know in my heart I'll see him again someday-
To this day I still have that porch swing-
When I sit in it alone, I can still feel him there-
Papa, I love you, always-
May God bless you and Meme, both-

His Name Is God

He comes from a distance that is so far-
But it is something how He knows where we all are-
He knows everything we do-
From when we are glad and happy or sad and blue-
If you just seek Him hard enough, He can send you
down the right path-
And help with life's disastrous aftermath-
He is in our present's every moment-
There is no need for an appointment-
He hides in the back of our minds, pay attention to
Him-
He knows you have the time-
Treat Him like your dearest friend-
And He will see you through to the end-
He can give us gifts we could never buy-
Like our health, His love, our love, the sun and
moon and natural things, like the stars in the sky-
He can mend our broken past-
And give us His love that will last-
He will patch a broken heart-
He plays the leading part-
He knows when every life should come to an end-
Because He wrote it when it began-
He can help you win your victory-
And show us so many new discoveries-
If you show Him love and devotion-

He will tend to your torn emotions-
He is the one who knows the even and odds-
He is the one we call "God"-

To Believe In One's Self

Believing in yourself is to love one's self as you
are-
It takes great courage, hope and strength to search
and find-
Go with this feeling of contentment and spread your
horizons-
There is a light shinning down for you, follow it-
One's compassion can take them down the path that
is right for them-
Hope for the path that will see you through-
Belief is in the eye of the seeker, so hold on to this
belief-
Believing in yourself can help you to become wise-
Wisdom of yourself is a gift you can be proud of-
Be like a baby and take the first step to just believe
in all you can become-
Work with your inner self, explore-
Look at what one's self can achieve-
Love yourself enough to believe in your heart to
take you to your goals-
It also takes confidence and pride that is deep down
inside all of us-
It is there, but it is up to you to want it bad enough
for you to have that power-
It is marvelous gift once it has been found-

Always remember to love and believe in yourself
That will be the reward you have won-

Splendor

You will surrender to my wondrous splendor-
I will amaze you with all I can do-
With the touch of just one hand you will
understand-
The feelings I can bring out in you, will be
something brand new-
The passion I feel for you is on a magical mission-
My splendor will endure you forever-
As you explode with that rush of adrenalin, it will
feel amazing-
You are what I need and been waiting for, you
make me want more-
I can blow your mind, just give me time-
I will bring you up as far as you want to go, this I
know-
This splendor that I feel is quite beautiful and so
real-
It wants your attention to show you what have been
missing-
Just see what uncovers when we are lovers-
It is no wonder we are like no others-
When we come together, it makes me want to fly-
And feels so good I could cry-
The splendor you make me feel causes my heart to
beat harder-

Erin Schenk

And I fall deeper into you and for you never had a
clue-
The sparkle I put into your eyes-
That is the greatest prize-
This I have known from the start-
I would win your heart-
It blows my mind that you can be gentle and kind-
And this I also know, you will always be mine-
There is a special splendor in you I fell in love with-
This is the love that will never surrender-

All of Me

I will give you all of me, my heart, and my soul,
everything-
I want to be the one you will run to, I can hold you-
Never wonder if I will always be there, I am
forever-
Don't worry I will love you with all of me-
I will give you the air I breathe it that is what you
need-
I promise you that my heart is something you will
never miss-
I will always be here for you, to give love, a hug
and a kiss-
I know you can never see me all at once-
But believe me I am here as one-
All of me needs all of you-
Because you are who I shine through-
To you, all of me can bring you such happiness-
And my love brings with it such kindness-
Love me, with all of you, this I know you can do-
All we both need is just to love you and me-

Erin Schenk

Sunset, Sunrise

Sunsets and sunrises can bring with them such
beauty-
They bring with them tranquility-
The sunset can help you forget your troubles-
You may feel yourself feeling more humble-
The sunrise will let you know it is time to rise-
The things you will see may come as a surprise-
Soak up the sun and watch things transform you
love-
With them they bring you healing and a sense of
well being-
Sunset means that it is almost time for you rest-
It is when the birds and other animals will nest-
Sunrise is when the world starts to awaken-
It's true their beauty can never be mistaken-
They are both unique and they are something we
could never make-

Restless Heart, Restless Mind

Restless heart, restless mind neither one knows the
time-
That restless heart climbs up an endless ladder-
While the restless mind listens to useless chatter-
The restless heart can be broke apart-
But as for the restless mind, it doesn't know where
to start-
With one you may feel weak-
But with the other it may have a slow leak-
One can't find where it belongs-
For the other it can't find what is wrong-
Both control the body and spirit-
Though they sometimes forget it-
For the restless heart it seems so helpless-
And as for the restless mind, can seem quite
useless-
They both may make you feel rejected-
Or sometimes make you feel unprotected-
They may cause you not to believe in miracles-
And cause you to go around in circles-
Be strong, so they do you no wrong-

Erin Schenk

Loving You

Loving you is right and true it is what I always
wanted to do-
You help keep me happy, instead of sad and blue-
You help me keep my feet on the ground-
I know you will always be around-
Loving you will keep me wise-
You are there in the morning when I rise-
You believing in me helps me to believe in you-
Our love for one another is so true and pure-
We can be each other's forever cure-
My heart will follow yours wherever it may lead-
To you I give this heart, you have freed-
Loving you is my heart's desire-
Your touch sets my body and soul on fire-
My one and only leading man-
By your side I will always stand-
Loving you is one of the qualities of being happy
with myself-
And my love will always be gratis to you-
In loving you, you have shown me who God really
is-
He is the one that brought us together-
For us to spend the rest of our lives loving each
other, forever-

Brighter Days

The sun is shinning and you should be smiling-
It is a spring morning and the flowers are blooming-
Hurry up and let's go-
We have a lot of exploring to do-
We are going to have a lot of fun-
We can laugh and run-
We can build sandcastles on the beach-
There are so many things that I can reach-
Brighter days are here to make you feel good-
Come on let's have fun just like I knew you could-
Make a fresh start-
Go with the feelings that comes from your heart-
We can play all day-
For your happiness I want it to stay-
Brighter days makes everything alright-
We are going, so hold on tight-
May you follow me to a wondrous land-
Where there are so many wonderful things at the
palm of your hand-
Dream of brighter days to come to you-
My days are brighter and happier now that my eyes,
I have open-
 For my brighter days have been carefully chosen-
Brighter days will occur when you find inner peace-
Before you know it you're heart will have release-

Touching You

Watching out the window as the rain falls-
We are wrapped up on a blanket as love calls-
My attention is focused on nothing, but you-
Confined to each other we are all we know-
Every time we touch I will let my love show-
Slow and sensual my touch will melt you like ice-
Rushed by the intensity of every feeling is warm
and nice-
As the petals of love fall all around us-
My heart is wherever you are, no need to fuss-
As I touch you I feel like I could reach the stars-
I know forever in my arms is where you are-
My mouth is dry, but I am not thirsty-
Captivated by your alluring and sensuous embrace
of intensity-
 The lasting satisfaction of your taste is on my lips-
My hands have no control of where they may slip-
Out of control are the fiery flames of desire-
The amount that I love you will never expire-
Touching you is exquisite sensation of my soul-
My passion for you will forever burn as hot as coal-
Just to remind you of how important you really are-
Just by my touch it will take you to the stars-
As my fingers run their course over every inch of
you-

My heartbeat and my touch will always be in love
with you-

Erin Schenk

Kids Have No Clue

Kids, kids, kids always to busy to stop-
They play until they feel like they'll drop-
They can be so hyper with too much sugar and pop-
Their obsession with cartoons-
Fascination with balloons-
Pulling pranks on mom, while dad plays along-
And knowing they can get in trouble when they do
wrong-
They don't know what life has in store for them-
But now they just want to have fun-
All they think about is laughing, playing and
running-
They have no idea that their later life is going to be
cunning-
They will have to fit in to get anywhere-
And before they know it, life has disappeared-
When they are adults they will have many difficult
decisions-
And be upset at what may come into their vision-
They will have to follow more directions-
And understand even more difficult instructions-
They want to grow up so fast-
And when they get older they wonder what happen
to the past-
They will have to work hard to get very far-
To realize that is who they are-
So kids don't grow up so fast-
That you want to live in the past-

My Heart's Gift

Translate my heart to your heart-
Connect all the lines-
That is yours and mine-
Bring it all together gently-
As for my love I have plenty-
I am ready to share-
I have all this love to spare-
I can give you all you'll ever need-
I can do it with grace and speed-
I will do this no matter where-
I know that my love will be there-
Smiling, because I know your heart belongs to
mine-
I know with these two hearts everything will be
fine-
My heart will love you now-
You will never have to ask "how"-
I have the strength to love you for so very long-
I hope I can always be this strong-
This I know without any mistake-
My love for you I will never fake-
And my gift from me to you-
Is this love that is so true-

Clean Me Up

Clean me up, I am a mess-
For I must look my best-
For tonight is the ball-
I have to look pretty for them all-
And all the merry men in their Mercedes Benz-
The dress I wear and my hair has to be perfect-
As I arrive in my limousine-
It is all amazing to me-
When I enter the room-
Everything and everyone is nice and groomed-
As everyone dances-
And throws each other glances-
From the streamers and flowers, it couldn't be any
fancier-
As the band plays-
We all dance and want to stay-
We eat and drink all the sweet treats-
And dance to the beat-
As the party goes on-
I want to dance all night long-
I don't want to be late-
Because tonight is going to be great-
So I must wake up and clean me up-
So I can go dance like I just dreamed-

Green Light, Means I Go

The green light means I go-
And to you is where I go-
I rush to you as fast as I can-
In your arms is where I will land-
And when the green light is shinning for me-
It means I better get ready-
With speed and grace I will go-
But sometimes I will take it steady and slow-
I reeve up my engine and I am pumped up with
fuel-
But you are my secret tool-
My gears are spinning and my heart is racing-
I am ready to roll, so just let me go-
Let me follow my own lead-
And take me to what I need-
My green light is waiting for me-
To take me to where I need to be-
That green light is my inspiration-
And it is full of anticipation-
With full speed ahead-
There is nothing I will dread-
I praise lavishly this green light I have been shown-
I will never delude what I have chosen-

Erin Schenk

My Heart

I was born with a hole in my heart-
But for some reason I was saved to play some
special part-
I went through a tremendous surgery at three
months old-
And died twice during surgery, I was told-
I had the fight in me, but God only knows why-
It's like a power booster that they had put in me-
Because when I was growing up, it was always on
high-
From then on I was on the moved at full speed-
No one could hardly keep up with me-
I never could sit still for more than five minutes-
From my four wheeler to my trampoline-
To being a tomboy to a dancing queen-
My heart was fully charged and ready for me-
I have the fight in me to never give up-
All I know by the end of the day everyone was tired
of keeping up- I even wore my dog out, named
Smokey-
But he wouldn't let me go anywhere that he wasn't
with me-
By the end of the day he was barely able to move-
He was one of the things that kept me going, but he
never had a clue-
But my heart is one I never want to live without-

It was built just for me, because it knows what I am
all about-
I thank God for my special heart that is mine-
Forever with God I will always feel fine-
I am fighter; He knew it from the start-
I know God loves me, every little part, including
my heart-
He has granted me the wisdom to enjoy my writing-
But somehow He has been beside me helping me
with the life I have been fighting-
I feel I have overcome so many difficult obstacles-
With my heart, it has made it all more possible-
I have this marvelous guardian angel still watching
over me-
I am thankful for the life and heart that has been
given to me-

Stay Away Sorrow

God is the only one that can help me with my
sorrow-
For your advice is some I don't want to borrow-
Though what is in my heart is what I need to
follow-
I will not ask you to stay-
But you can do this for me, just pray-
I promise I will make it through my day-
I am the one that feels so hurt-
For I don't know what I say, I just blurt-
Some things in my vision have no meaning or
reason-
Just sometimes I wonder who I am pleasing-
I have been knocked down so many times-
Some things have been so unkind-
One instinct I have learned is sometimes, I have to
give up-
Because I know in the end I will erupt-
I know I am not designed to be that angry-
It just for a little knowledge, I am hungry-
I shouldn't woollier in self-pity or over indulge-
Because at the seams I may bulge-
God, I know you are the one that can pick me up-
To get my head and my heart out of this slump-
I know you will be there, if I just ask-
To end the sorrow and help me accomplish my task-

The sorrow I have will not stick around long-
Before I know it, it will be gone-

Erin Schenk

Beauty Is All Around

To be able to look at a painting and see what the
artist saw-
It is the beauty that they saw within their mind-
Beauty is all around you, but not too many stop to
pay attention long enough-
There is beauty in the way shadows appear when
the sun shines through a window-
A mountain is the most breath taking with its forms,
colors and shades-
An old church with its peaks, steeples, and the color
of the cut glass windows-
The trees as the wind blows them, the sounds they
make and the different shapes they take as they
bend with the breeze-
The birds singing outside in one of the softest
sounds that could ever be heard-
God put so many beautiful things in this world that
people overlook to often-
The flowers, the structure of the mountains, all the
different shapes of natural things, that man could
never make-
The seas and all the creatures among the waters and
all the animals that are among the land-
But you will not see the beauty in anything if you
do not look beyond what you have already seen-

Winter, Spring, Summer and Fall

Winter is when everything is at rest, from flowers to
trees and even some animals-
Winter is also the season to stay indoors and be
closer to the ones you love-
Spring is when everything starts to come back to
life and becomes one of the most beautiful seasons
to appear-
Spring is also the time to get out and plant a tree or
plant a garden-
Summer is the time to enjoy swimming, cold
lemonade, picnics and the smell of flowers
blooming-
Summer is one of the seasons that you enjoy with
your family and friends-
Fall is when the colors begin to change into reds,
yellows and oranges; everything is getting ready for
the long winter rest-
Fall is also a time to take a long walks in the park
and to enjoy life outdoors-
And the winter is here with it's cold winds, falling
in temperatures, and the snow-
The winter reminds us to stay warm and not catch a
cold-
But spring is right around the corner before you it
with its beautiful array of wonders-

Erin Schenk

And spring is when the animals come back out from
sleeping and are glad it is spring-
Summer is here to let us know that heat still exist at
least one season out of the year-
It is the time for baseball games and hotdogs at the
park-
Fall is not far behind with its changing way to let
everything know that it is time for another rest-
All the seasons come and go every year without
fail-
If everything else in life could be this predictable,
there would be an inner peace among all-

Tomorrow Is Another Day

People always say tomorrow, but today give praise-
Today is here and it is yours, why wait-
Start your life the way you want to live it today-
Don't wait until tomorrow, it maybe to late-
Today open the doors of where you want to go, if
you wait for tomorrow, you may never know-
Tomorrow may never come, so take today in a full
run-
Tomorrow is another day, so start living for today-
Life is a race, but slow down today and take your
own pace-
Today shouldn't be so complicated you have to
worry about tomorrow-
Don't lock away what you can solve or do today-
Give thanks and except the circumstances you face
everyday-
Today break that silence and say what you need to
say-
And don't wait until tomorrow to tell that someone
you love them, tell them today-
Just think to yourself, tomorrow may or may not
come, so stop running for the future-
The present is what you have don't try to look any
further-

Erin Schenk

Think of Today

Can you think of what you can accomplish in this
day-
Maybe taking a few minutes to stop and pray-
Helping the ones that you love and the ones you
should-
Being happy with where you are and not where you
could-
Today seeing how many lives you can change-
And stop looking at life and people as if they are
strange-
Be there for someone who needs you most-
And try to be a good host-
Take inventory of all your personal glory-
Tell someone a special kind of love story-
Just to be proud you have the air you breathe-
And pay attention to the person you are deep
beneath-
Today search for the place you really need to be-
And to be thankful for just being you and me-

Life Ahead

Stop what you are doing-
Where do you thing you are going-
You better not go in there-
Be quiet and stay right here-
I'll protect you from what is ahead-
It can hit you like a ton of lead-
It don't care who you are-
You just think it can take you far-
Sometimes it may make you feel good-
But it is dangerous, understood-
It can play tricks on your mind-
And make you think that the world is kind-
It will knock you down so hard-
It can knock you a hundred yards-
It can make fun of you-
And sometimes make you feel you are no use-
At times it can bring you down-
And other times you just want to drown-
Never knowing what is in store, peace or an uproar-
It may cause you to drink-
And be so confusing you don't know what to think-
It can slam you against the door-
And cause you to crawl on the floor-
You may fall to your knees, while begging please-
While it comes at you day after day-
And may led you astray-

Life can go better if you just stop for a minute and
Pray-
Life will go ahead with it's course-
And there are parts that are going to be better or
Worse-
All we can do is try to control our own lives-
While others do what they can for their lives-

Strange Thoughts

Wow, you have entered again, what I am going to
do about you-
You are always there causing me to say the
strangest things-
Get away from me; you have got to be crazy-
The weirdest things seem to happen when you come
around-
The way I act, the way I think, the way I speak and
the words I use-
I feel so not me when you are near, leave me alone-
You are doing this all to amuse yourself, not me-
You come around when ever you feel like it,
bugging me-
I have no use for you, so why do you keep coming
around-
All you do is confuse me of what I am suppose to
be doing-
I just can't get it through to you; I don't want you-
I can be thinking perfectly happy thoughts and here
you come-
You make me think of the craziest things ever-
Go away; don't come into my head, never-
You step into my mind whenever you feel like it's
the time-
I am tired of you, you are useless-
Strange thoughts be gone, I don't want you hanging
out-

Erin Schenk

The Painting

The painting on the wall could see it all-
It could hear the shouts coming from down the hall-
For this was an unusual painting, it could see and
hear-
And it was hanging in an unusual house, one of
fear-
It would watch as the most terrible things would
happen-
For anyone who entered the house would be trapped
in-
And the painting, it was so very old-
It has seen this house be very cold-
It has heard things being torn apart-
For it knows every horrible sound by heart-
The face in the painting is alive-
It has seen so many things that never survive-
It hangs in a house that is forever haunted-
For the spirits that live there can never be taunted-
The painting will be around to see much more-
And see things no one else has seen before-

His Friend

As he slowly opened the door-
There she lay face down on the floor-
He cried this awful whine-
He screamed, "why did this have to happen to mine"-
She lay there silent and still-
He felt helpless and thought, "this can't be real"-
For the woman he loved had been killed-
Someone did it just for the thrill-
How could someone be so evil-
The person must work for the devil-
He heard about a killer who was on the loose-
Who like to choke his victims with a noose-
As he walked around his wife, he saw the rope around her neck-
And he noticed the door was open that lead to the deck-
He called his best friend at the police department-
They couldn't find him anywhere, not even at his apartment-
He never realized his friend had a hidden secret-
A year ago his wife mysteriously disappeared-
His friend was a lot worse then he thought-
His friend had split personalities-
But until his wife was killed it wasn't a reality-
Now she is dead and he can't be found-
His heart is so hurt it can't even pound-

Portrait of Love

The portrait of love is a precious one-
It holds a beauty all it's own-
The picture of love can be so cherished-
One is a child holding on to their special treasure-
They can be life's simple pleasures-
That picture is forever in your mind-
The portrait of love is warm and kind-
It can make you feel lucky you have this love-
The one you hang high above-
God is the perfect portrait of love-
The picture of love is one you are happy to see-
This picture will shine with happiness and glee-
The portrait of love can say a thousand words-
And it can sing a thousand chords-
This picture can coordinate with us all-
It will one day be the most important one to fall-

Blessed Is You

Blessed are you, Heavenly Father, who looks from
afar-
In the sky you placed every single star-
With your companion, mother nature-
You two set out for quite adventure-
While you hung the moon-
She made the flowers that bloom-
You both work together to make everything-
And your creations are so amazing-
Every fish in the sea has their own story-
While the trees rise to a higher glory-
As you both made every plant imaginable-
She is the one that made them manageable-
The gift you gave of every hour-
And the scents she gave every flower-
If it wasn't for you, two, we wouldn't exist-
You are the ones who deserve heavenly bliss-
But on the seventh day you looked at what you
accomplished and were amazed-
No one could give the gifts you gave-
You are the reason we exist and live-

Erin Schenk

A Child's Plea

I am too young to understand-
I just want someone to hold my hand-
I get scared when I am left alone-
Why can't you call me on the phone-
Am I the reason you are going away-
Did I do something, that's why you won't stay-
Please answer me, I want to know-
Oh, please don't leave me, please don't go-
I promise I'll be good-
I'll mind you like I should-
Don't go and leave me like this-
For your company I will miss-
Daddy, you can't, this can't be-
You still have so much to teach me-
We never took that camping trip-
You forgot to sign my permission slip-
We are suppose to go to the zoo next week-
From mama worrying about you, she is losing
sleep-
Get out of that bed and lets go home-
Come on, I want you to take me to get a ice cream
cone-
You missed my little league game-
I scored a touchdown and the crowd went insane-
I have been talking to you; you haven't even
blinked an eye-
Oh, please daddy don't you die-
That would just make mama cry-

And I am not ready to say goodbye-
I know you don't want to leave us now-
Come on you can fight it some how-
I still have a lot of growing up for you to see-
And remember two weeks from now is my spelling
bee-
You said you wouldn't do this to me-
You told me you still have lots of time before you
leave-
The doctors told mama your heart is not strong
enough anymore-
They don't know how much longer you have,
they're not for sure-
I am only seven you aren't suppose to leave me yet-
I know you'll get better, I just bet-
I prayed every night before I went to bed-
But I guess they didn't get answered because now
you are dead-
They did all they could do to help-
When they told mama you died, she just yelled-
As for me, I just sat there by myself-
Like one of my toys on a shelf-

I, Am Charmed

There is a princess that could never be charmed-
So many suitors came to call on her to walk with
her arm and arm- She was never satisfied with any
of the men-
Her parents, the king and queen didn't know when
her pickiness would end-
Many were suitable enough to wear the royal
crown-
They couldn't seem to make her happy with anyone
they brought around-
So disappointed they couldn't find Prince Charming
for their daughter-
Until one day the princess was riding in the forest
on her horse-
When there was one of the most handsome knights
riding the same course-
He saw her and thought to himself, " he never saw a
more beautiful sight"-
She saw him and knew that he was just right-
He came up and introduced himself and bowed and
kissed her hand-
Her breath was taken away by the charm in this
man-
She thought to herself, "he is perfect, the one I am
going to marry"-
She told him her name was, "Princess Mary"-

He said, "I am charmed to meet you, I am Sir
Knight Cameron"- He helped her down from her
horse and they walked together for awhile-
He could make her laugh and immediately fell in
love with her smile-
It was love at first sight for these two-
She took him back to the palace to meet her parents-
She told them, "he is the one for me, I feel so
happy"-
Her parent's faces light up with joy-
And her father said, "I see you have made your
choice"-
Her mother commented, " I am glad you have found
the right man"-
Now you have someone to walk with you hand and
hand-
For when you turn twenty-one, you will become
queen-
For we hope you and him will be a successful king
and queen-
Your father and I will soon be handing my crown
over to you-
We are glad you found someone that will be
suitable just for you-
Sir Knight Cameron will soon be king and you my
dear will be queen-
May you do justice as I have done, if you do, you
will shine and gleam-
Are you ready to be the next king and queen-

Soul Searching

The soul is silent, but says many words-
It is connected to you forever-
They can become lost, found never-
It brings you closer to how you are-
As it lays just under the surface-
Believe that it is always with you-
They live in us our whole lives-
It is the reality in us-
We sometimes break the convent we have with it-
We should listen to it when we need to do the right
thing-
It lets us know we are doing fine-
For it searches your whole life for you-
It needs rest for it to go on-
But there are so many out there that are lost-
And that are torn apart and forgotten-

Peace of Mind

This peace of mind can help you to remain calm-
The sense of tranquility it can send-
That peace of mind can be an everlasting friend-
It can help you keep your focus-
It's habit of keeping what is important to you close-
The things it can help you see-
And all you need is this peace-
It can help keep everything under control-
This peace of mind can bring to you what you need-
Will not let you ponder or feel greed-
It is the key to serenity and security-
And washes away any impurities-
But keep this in mind; you have to make peace with
yourself-
So it can all work together for it's self-

Want To Be

As the darkness falls upon the land-
A peculiar smell lingers through the air-
For as far as you could see the trees formed a band-
In this place the weather was quite fare-
You could hear the wind sing it's song-
The sweet smell of rain was all around-
For it had just rained all day long-
This is the most pleasant place I have ever found-
As the sun was going down and dusk was sitting in-
For the crickets start to play their silhouettes-
As for the night slowly set in and tranquility of rest
begin-
Bring me, my salvation like a roaring jet-
Let every creature be at peace-
For this is where I want to be-

Protect Me

They approach me silently-
They surround me, completely-
They were sent to watch over me-
For they knew I needed thee-
My enemy was coming at me fast-
They knew I would not last-
They protect me from all sides-
For with my enemy, they will collide-
I knew they would help me save myself-
They helped me escape the evil-
With them I was not afraid-
By my side is where they stayed-
As I stayed balanced and strong-
I knew they would not treat me wrong- I was
focused and sure-
For their loyalty to me was pure-
My guardian angels that are here-
I know will always be near-

Demolished World

As I pass the people walking by, they don't even
say "hi"-
 Rudeness has become the way of the world-
Everyone is out for themselves and don't care about
anyone else-
Paying no attention to someone in need, all they
think, "is poor little me"-
Living in debt up to their throat, hanging
themselves with an invisible rope-
Cradling themselves in the comforts they can't
afford-
Looking for someone else to pay the room and
board-
Driving a new car, their not any better off than the
poor people are-
Living in these new houses that are way to small-
It wouldn't be enough room for me to live
comfortably at all-
The Sunday Christians, gossip during the week after
they leave church-
Putting themselves on a pedestal or high on a perch-
Half the world is fake and that makes all the
fairytales look good-
So many have come to misinterpret God and He is
misunderstood-
The doubtfulness in this world comes out more
Everyday-

There are things I would rather not see, in my house
I would rather stay-
Keep to myself and just let the world fall apart-
I know it eventually will, deep down in my heart-
I'd rather clean the mess that is in my home-
Than to be cleaning up after people have roamed-
I'd rather deal with the pain and anguish that goes
on in my own little world-
For God has tried so many times to help us, but we
demolished our own world-
We have become the enemies of ourselves-
Wondering why we have to live through all this
hell-
For the world is just leased to us and our time is
about up-

Tragedy

Oh, tragedy don't come around us today-
You bring things with you that won't go away-
Wherever you go disaster follows-
And bringing other things that makes us feel
hallow-
Sometimes fate will bring you along-
To help us grow and be strong-
You come at us fast-
Hit people with a hard blast-
You keep yourself at a far distance-
You can arrive at any instant-
You catch people off guard-
You take a mile when you are only given a yard-
You take people and things away from us-
 And cause mental abuse-
You try to break our spirit and cause us to loss-
You scheme and plan to grind us in the sand-
Hoping we can't catch ourselves with both hands-
You change our lives with your visits-
With your disastrous acts, that you exhibit-
Take yourself somewhere else-
Stop making us feel helpless-
The suffering you bring-
Cause us to cry and scream-
It is no doubt at sometimes you will come about-
We never hear you coming-
You are silently bounding and drumming-
We know you are something we can't control-

Except to make it through and take our hold-
We know you will always be around-
All we can do is not let you bring us down-
The world cannot condemn you; because you are
part of our lives-
Sometimes you may change what is wrong in our
lives-
To help us realize that we do not have it so bad-
But sometimes you can cause us to be so sad-
You are here to let us know that we must develop
and grow-
At times you will hit us in the head and try to strike
us with your blow-
You can bring everything down on us at once-
Because you have that big of a punch-
Sometimes you cause us to hide or crawl-
All we want to do is make it through your fall-
You try to cause pain and hurt, above all you just
want to be heard-
You can cause us to be confused and scared-
You hide yourself well, but you will always be
there-
Just waiting somewhere-
Tragedy, I know you are not a enemy, just one of
the natural things-

Don't Invade Me

You come sweeping in like a ghost in the night-
Causing me to have this terrible fright-
But you will not dare show your face-
You come into my mind and take up space-
Looking forward to playing games with my mind-
For your acts of playing are not kind-
You ravish yourself in making me feel bad-
That you are happy when I am sad-
You like to see me get frustrated and cry-
I can't get through to you, you won't say goodbye-
You kick me down when I want to run-
I know you stick around just for fun-
You will not bend, you will not break-
All you want is to fill my life full of mistakes-
I would like to elude from your life-
Because you keep cutting me like a knife-
You never pardon yourself for very long-
Trying to make me weak when I want to stay
strong-
And you delude me every time you get a chance-
You ram my heart and leave me in a trance-
You are no avail to me, so please leave-
I know you are the one who will always deceive-

Outlines In My Mind

I scramble through my day-
Always looking for a better way-
The outlines in my mind won't let me see clearly-
Everything seems to come, severely-
My eyes begin to cloud up with tears-
I am hoping they will wash away my fears-
The lump in my throat will not let me speak-
For my conscience, is at it's peak-
The night falls upon me slowly-
Those days come back daily-
And I run for safety-
I can control more of the bad things, lately-
My head is spinning me around-
But my inner peace, I have found-
I will change the outlines in my mind for good-
Try not to look back on my childhood-

Fortunate To Be Loved

The fortune of your love, is my best luck-
With you, is where I'd rather be stuck-
I am the richest when I am loved by you-
You are my addiction that I can't get enough of-
I gamble my every feeling just to win your love-
The anticipation of winning your heart is what I was
out for-
You are the fortune I wanted to love, I couldn't help
it, and I wanted more-
So close your eyes and think about the way I make
you feel-
I am permanent high that you know is real-
The twinkle in my eye is the fortune you have
found-
I took my risk and caused you to float off the
ground-
You swept me away when you won my heart-
I knew you were the one who was going to top the
chart-
We can be players that will always win each other-
Because we know in our hearts there will never be
another-
The most fortunate thing for you, is you are always
loved-

Impressed

Impressed, look I have done it again-
I can't help it, you cause it-
My intuition goes haywire when you are around-
It tells me to love you and that's what I do-
But that is okay, because that is a good thing-
I am impressed because I can feel like this-
I don't feel I am in a constant mess-
So head in my direction, I want to impress you-
This impression I'll leave on you, will astonish you-
It can cause you to misbehave, impressive, uh! -
This game of impression is one I will play-
Because I know I can get your attention-
I am going to win this game, honey-
Don't worry, I am impressed, you participated-
You can't fight it, you can't hide it, you are
impressed-

Erin Schenk

Dancer In Me

The dancer in me has always felt free-
I can move my body so gracefully-
I can dance to any beat, just watch me-
I move across the floor-
In my youth I could dance for hours behind my
bedroom door-
I have been dancing since I could walk-
Using dancing as my method, while other people
rather talk-
Just put some music on and I will go-
Just by myself, not wanting to put on a show-
The way I dance is with the music up loud and
without a crowd-
Dancing makes me feel so good, with my body in
motion-
I need no reason to be in the notion-
From every move, step and breath I take, is the
dancer in me-
I know I don't have to pretend to be the dancer I
could be-
I move with ease as if I am weightless-
There is not a part of me that is not motionless-
I don't need a stage to do what I can perform-
I'll move with the grace of lighting like in a storm-
As the sweat runs down my face-
My heart will run it's race-
As I lie breathless on the floor-
The dancer in me is tired once more-

Tangled Imagination

I am tangled up in an imagination that has been lost-
For it has been tied in such hard knots-
The contrast of it's hope is buried and gone-
It can't create with what is left, it is done-
It searches for an image, but finds nothing-
Though it tries so hard to seek something-
It can't make sense of what it does see-
It's as if the mind has found a way to flee-
Trying to open up, but it is tangled in a web-
Fighting and struggling to get free of this web-
Not able to think clearly of a happy moment-
Going insane trying to find some kind of
confinement-
Where it can be comfortable and work again-
Finding away out so a new life can begin-
Wanting to create all it can with a new found
wisdom-
Untangling it's self from this difficult prism-
Finding a place where it knows it has been before-
Where it had the freedom to do its will and so much
more-
Not fully aware of where it should go now that it is
almost free-
Doing all it can to just be apart of me-
It goes where I go everyday-
I can't leave it behind and it likes it that way-
Helping me change the things I know I can become-
For I need to use it all and not just some-

My imagination is one thing I never want to be
tangled up-
Because if it wasn't for it, I couldn't be the person I
love-

Crisis

A shinning light that guides us through the crisis-
The armored shield that protects us from our fears-
The burning in our eyes, sees the secrets of
ourselves-
Looking for a future, but only seeing the minute
ahead-
Jumping from life to life and not being able to reach
anything- Smiling, when full of depression and
crying inside-
Hoping one day you have something to smile about-
Losing someone close to you forever and never
seeing them again-
Blaming yourself for things that others have done to
you-
One day you will face the truth and know it wasn't
your fault-

Erin Schenk

God's Ring of Hope

God is the true ring of hope-
He will never be the one to slope-
He can perform many of our hopeless miracles-
He can help our hopes from running in circles-
He can bring to our life the simplest pleasures-
One's that we can always treasure-
His ring of hope is something that is given to all of
us-
If you just believe you will not stumble or fall-
He can guide us to where we need to go-
God can make a masterpiece out of hope-
He will give it to you anytime you need-
Just be patient, wait and see-
The ring of hope lives in all of us-
And it is God who we should always trust-

All I Need

Traveling down a winding road-
With no particular place to go-
Just to be with you is all I need-
You take your time and never speed-
You will take me anywhere I wish-
My love for you is so very rich-
We pretend we are the only two in the world-
I listen to every little word-
We are fascinated with everything around-
We park and lay a blanket on the ground-
We stare at the sky-
And we watch the planes fly by-
With nothing on our minds but being together-
And wishing this could go on forever-
As the breeze sends the smell of sweet flowers-
And the trees shade us as if they are towers-
You hold me close and kiss me gently-
For I have all I need, I have plenty-
I let go of my control-
So glad you are the one I hold-
From now on you are all I need-

2 Erin Schenk

Four Letter Word

Play me sweet songs of love-
Hold me tonight, make love-
I know you are the one, I truly love-
The sweetest word you say is, "love"-
 All over again I would fall in love-
In my heart, I know how much I love-
Cradled in your arms, I feel love-
My happiness is in love-
With you I am in love-
You are my amber of love-
My favorite four letter word is "love"-

The Battle Won

You are enslaved by your body, mind and soul-
This incredible power comes over you and takes
hold-
Bursting forth with the unstoppable, rush of
adrenaline-
Your energy level goes far beyond it's limit-
You are beating like a drum from the element of
excitement- Racing through your body is your
blood boiling, entrapment-
Increasing that person inside you that has to come
forward-
Throwing your head back as everything inside of
you moves upward-
You feel you could fly all around the world and
never stop-
The burning that makes you want to go all the way,
all the way to the top-
Creating a glory for yourself that no one else can
touch-
Killing that beast that has held you back from so
much-
Crawling out of the hole you put yourself in-
Screaming because you know in that hole is where
it all began-
Realizing you were chasing yourself around in the
dark-
Coming into the light that has a most dazzling and
magnificent spark-

Significantly the most exquisite thing inside you,
you will ever see-
Battlement with your soul for the fulfillment of
something that can be-
Like a sword piercing you and slowly being pulled
back out-
This strength comes over you and takes over and
you start to understand what this is all about-
 Realizing you are screaming at the top of your
lungs and know you have been heard-
You start spinning yourself out of control, these
pictures dance inside your head-
This urge causes you to claw at the air, wanting to
scratch some kind of surface-
Guarding with this silver shield at your chest as you
take your place-
Battling and defeating the enemy that has tried to
attack and you watching them fall-
You exhibit your nobility and bravery and show
them all-
As your enemy lies on the ground pawning for any
gasp of air-
They are slowly dying from the punctures they
acquired and just lie there-
As you are shouting your, hurray of victory-
Clenching your fist and shouting "I have won over
my misery"-
You celebrate your declaration of victory, while
your enemies' lay in the field, dead-

As you wipe their blood from your face and never
bow your head-
For you have accomplished that battle that your
Enemy inflicted on you-
You know you have given your self a gift that is
True-

Erin Schenk

The Gifts

The gift of air that helps us exist-
The gift of gossip we can't resist-
The gift to reach our every desire-
And the wondering why it feels like inside of us is a
burning fire-
The gift of controlling our temptations-
And the creations of our imaginations-
The gift of sight so we can see what is all around-
And the food that nourishes us that comes from the
ground-
The gift of laughter so we can be happy-
And the helping of getting through things that are
saddening-
The gifts that in due time we will receive everything
we need-
And the Lord's courage that He gives us to succeed-

Free Spirit

I have this free spirit like no other-
It is full of passion and fire-
 Running with the freedom in my heart-
But I didn't feel this way from the start-
It took time for all of this to come out-
The freedom of my spirit moves all about-
Like the spirits of wild horses, running free-
That is the kind of spirit that lives in me-

Erin Schenk

Reminding Myself

I always have to remind myself to do this, do that-
And to remind myself in the winter to put on my
hat-
There are times I forget where I am at-
Wondering if I even have a clue-
And remember to put the cap back on the glue-
 I remind myself everyday to tie my shoes-
For I am only a kid practicing what to do-
I can't believe I have to remember so many things-
Just trying to remember and the confusion it brings-
I remind myself to do my homework-
While everyone else reminds me, I am just a squirt-
I am reminded sometimes I am to little-
For I should just go run, play and piddle-
I am just a kid, how am I suppose to remember it
all-
Just remind yourself sometimes I am just to small-

Do It All

I sleep with my head under the covers-
I am just a kid scared of the lightening and thunder-
The booms and bangs make me jump every time-
I am allowed to be scared, I am only five-
As it gets louder I run down the hall and jump in
bed with mommy and daddy-
With them to protect me, I am safe and happy-
My older brother calls me a big baby-
But daddy told me he use to do the same thing-
When the morning comes I am glad my parents are
there-
For there will be many things in my life I'll fear-
I know with their help I can do it all-

Erin Schenk

Panic

As I lie there and cry to myself, I realize it is for
nothing-
To ponder with my mind to try to find some little
something-
Interrupted by the intense threshing of something
else going on inside my head-
No, not another one of these thoughts that should've
been buried and dead-
They are the ghosts and shadows that entrap my
memory-
They evolve with all the other burdens and pains I
carry-
A rage that takes over my body and blinds me from
seeing-
Blacking out and no knowledge of where I may go-
Uncontrollable shaking and shivers that take over-
As I sweat and are burning up, than suddenly I
become cold-
And it feels as if the fear is scratching and pawing
away at my stomach-
I become dizzy and feel I am spinning, my head
aches-
The urge to scream, but when I open my mouth
nothing comes out-
I feel my heart beating out of control, I just want to
shout-

Not being able to breathe, feels like I am
suffocating-
I start to feel faintness and having chills, not being
able to say anything-
It comes over me when I least expect it, it just takes
over me-
Clenching its jaws into me and not letting me free-
Passing out and seeing the people who love me are
trying to kill me-
I run, they just keep chasing me; they will not let
me be-
It is the panic that lives deep in my soul-
Using me for its sanctuary of control-
I wake up screaming, wondering where I am at-
And finally realizing it was just another panic
attack-

Erin Schenk

Trapped No More

I am awake, but still asleep-
For my mind is what is in the deep-
Everything in my mind is dark-
Like my mind is in permanent park-
I've drowned myself with mental anguish-
My memory has been squished-
My mind has had a sub-mental crash-
My thoughts are just filled with trash-
Through my teen years this how I felt-
I was torturing myself with a mental belt-
Whipping my packed away thoughts-
Traveling down the wrong track, I would get
caught-
But now I have foreseen that track-
There is no way in hell I am going back-
To go through my past again, I would be a fool-
My life now is pleasantly full-
 Trapped no more, I will be of what happened to
me-

Power Crush

A heart of steal with the will-
Passion of fire that burns with desire-
A captivated sight that had the fight-
A wondering soul is never whole-
Lights in the eyes of the blind-
Pulling together the ties that bind-
Changing the way of what you say-
Driven by a force that is course-
An adrenaline of wildness, rushes-
Together with power, it crushes-
Slapped with reality with a hard blow-
As your energy drains slow-
When you feel you are in a trance-
Throwing away every possible chance-
Catastrophic turmoil, boiling hot-
The power moves like a fast shot-

Pleasing You

As I lie naked next to you and feel your warm
caress-
I have decided I want you and nothing less-
As our lips meet, I know you are my favorite treat-
When I taste your skin-
I know exactly where to begin-
As I move slow-
Those sweet juices start to flow-
When you light my fuse, I burn like fire-
I will be your every desire-
You melt from my touch-
Because you want me that much-
Shh! I have all you need, I am sweet like honey-
You will see I am more valuable then money-
I want to touch you all I can-
You are all my man-
I whisper how much I want you-
And remind you, I love you-
I want to be close-
On you I will overdose-
I can be everything you expected-
There will be nothing I do I will regret-
My excursion is that I want to please you-

Ambers of Love

The ambers of the fire burn bright-
As we lay out under the sky, tonight-
The stars are hung just in the right spots-
The wind lightly blows the tree tops-
And the moon is full of life-
Created by a warmth of everlasting love-
The night sings to us as we hold each other close-
We light up in this night and feel no loss-
We know the ambers of our love will always glow-
For we know how to help our love grow-

Erin Schenk

The Step Mom, You Didn't Have To Be

I thank you for being the step mom I didn't expect
you to be-
You were kind and generous, always willing to help
me-
From the first time I met you, I knew I would
become close to you- You were the first one that
truly helped me open my heart to God- You treated
me more like your daughter, you made me feel
cherished-
You were there when I needed someone the most;
to me you will always be treasured-
You had the confidence in me that I would have
never found by myself-
And I found a friend in you, I couldn't find in
anyone else-
You spent time with me to try and help me and held
me when I would cry so much-
You made me feel secure and loved just by your
touch-
You were there for me during my teenage years
when I felt my life was such a mess-
Maybe God knew you were the one I needed then to
get me through my stress-
You helped me get over my phobia of driving and
taught me how-
 I hope you know how much you meant to me then
and now-

I know I really screwed up the last couple months I
was living at home-
Staying out all night, worrying you and you scared
of where I may roam-
I hope you know how sorry I am for what I put you
through-
I know dad was worried a lot, too-
I appreciate all that you brought into my life when
you were part of my life-
You did things for me I never expected you to do-
For some reason you were one of the major
stepping stones, I needed in my life then-
I am just glad in that time in my life when I needed
someone, you were my friend-
Through it all you were never mean, I hope you
know I will always love you, by all means-
You were the mom you didn't have to be and that
will always mean so much to me-

The Love Of A King and Queen

I lay there in the realm of darkness with my
imagination roaming-
I can't sleep, my dreams are my weakness and my
visualization is short-coming-
The visions I encounter, they are quite an
excitement-
Me, as a fairytale queen and feeling of
enchantment-
My royal king sits beside me upon his royal throne-
We are like one body from our minds and ideas, to
our flesh and bones-
One cannot function without the other by their side-
For both of us are together for this long ride-
As of one world we are planning a future that we
will never part-
 His breath is my breath and my heart is his heart-
For all love that we will make will keep us strong-
To put forth the effort of our magical love that can't
go wrong-
And to our sweet hereafter bond that will never be
broken-
For we are each other's treasure of this love that has
spoken-
To rule over the people as we rule over each other-
For we will never be a king and queen that will
search for another-
And as for our bed we share, will never be full of
plunder-

Let our love be the way to that inside thunder-
May the walls come crashing down before our love
will ever die-
As we lay there in the ruins side by side-
For when they find us, may they bury us as one-
For you are the one I love and to no other will I give
my love-

Erin Schenk

Lord Is Welcome

My lips are sealed-
For my heart you have healed-
The sweetness in all you do-
Is why I fell in love with you-
You are the God that is like no other-
For if I follow you, I can go further-
You have the mightiest power in all of heaven-
For you are the reason I am here-
And as for everyone else you are the one they
should fear-
Lord you have the strength of all men-
But you can be as gentle as a soft wind-
You gave me the gift of my senses-
And see me through my chances-
You are the one that will stand the most high-
You will never cheat me or lie-
I know you will walk with me when I need you
most-
And rid me of all my ghost-
I will claim you as my own-
You are welcomed anytime in my home-

Accept Life

Some sleep to avoid the signs of life approaching-
Cradling, themselves in their slumber of
disappearing-
Not looking out the front door to see what awaits-
Afraid of the world's and their own mistakes-
Knowing they have always been rejected or pushed
aside- Standing in the middle of a crowd, but still
alone-
Being made fun of or just left out-
Hiding from themselves and everyone else-
Not realizing they have a purpose for being here-
Creating an image in their mind of how it is suppose
to be-
And not accepting that this is exactly how it is
suppose to be-
Accept it, live it, enjoy it, appreciate it, love it,
embrace it, life-

Erin Schenk

The Doll on the Shelf

I have been sit up on this shelf and forgotten-
What's wrong with me, have I turned rotten-
I never get to go where she goes anymore-
She just walks past me and goes right out her
bedroom door-
I remember the fun we use to have, she use to take
me, everywhere-
When she was tucked into bed, she wouldn't go to
sleep without me there-
When she would go to school, I sat on her bed and
waited for her-
She would put me in the basket on her bike so I
could go with her-
All the tea parties and happy times together, how I
remember-
I know she is a teenager now, not interested in
playing with dolls-
When I see her now; she is on the phone for hours
with whom ever calls-
And interested in other things, like boys, friends and
malls-
I have watched her grow-up for the last six years
sitting on this shelf-
I wonder if she even knows I am here-
I haven't been played with in so many years-
She'll be going off to college soon, I'll probably be
left behind-

She is graduating in a week and has already started
packing everything she can find-
It is the day she is getting ready to leave, she has
packed her car-
 But wait, she runs back into her room, grasps me
and says to me, "without you I wouldn't have made
it this far"-
I am not going away without you and you have been
the one that has always been true-
So happy now that I haven't been forgotten and
knowing she still needs me-
Before she gets in the car, she puts me right in the
front seat-
Then she hugs her parents' goodbye, with tears
running down her face-
When she gets in and she says to me, "you will be
what keeps me close to this place"-

Watch For What You Dream

To sleep through the night as the hours pass-
And torn between the nightmares that surpass-
Then to wake yourself to find out it was just a
dream-
And the things you seen, makes you want to
scream-
The realistic scheme of it all makes it feel so real-
The art of the way a dream works and the way it
makes you feel-
Your thoughts can control the things you dream-
They can make things come to life, so it seems-
There are some that can cause such pain and crying-
Especially the ones when you see someone you
love, is dying-
Awaken in gloom of some kind of solitary
darkness-
Or recapture the realism of your dreams of
awareness-
You don't sleep because you are afraid of the
dreams that may come-
And the terrorizing feeling that it could be the last
one-
Becoming a warrior of your own dreams-
And the light that shines like a blinding beam-
They may take you to a far away land you don't
want to go-
Or show you things you really didn't want to know-

There are ones that can destroy the good ones you
have-
There maybe one that makes you feel your life has
been torn in half-
If we are happy and content, our dreams will be the
same-
And if we are frightened or sad, all they do is show
us shame-

Wings of Love

I fly on the wings of love that lead start to you-
I left up my heart to the skies you live above-
I know with me you share unconditional love-
If I just ask for your protection, you will protect me-
You made me the person I should always be-
The wings of your love will always be there-
One day I'll be carried from this world to yours-
Now you give me time to grow, breathe, and love
and live-
It is something how you have so much to give-
Untangling my mind with infinite wisdom-
The wings of your love is your created prism-
God the majestic maker of the wings of love-
He extends them to everyone that He loves-
The magic and power these wings carry-
The exuberance too never envy-
His wings are extended to the whole world-
Sheltering us from the other world of darkness and
evil-
Living in the existence of God will always be a
challenge to the devil-
For the devil flies with the wings of sin, but the
Lord flies with the wings of love-

Precious Love

Created in the light I hold-
For it is not hot or cold-
Is a love that will surpass all time-
Made with sense and beauty in mind-
It is sewn together like a quilt-
And has no need to carry guilt-
It is a love made for everyone-
I gave this precious love to my only son-

Comprehended Torture

One hides themselves in the deep, dark corner of
their mind- Increasingly unsure of what part of life
they belong-
Out casting of self and abandoning what their self
is-
Not consciously paying attention to what is in them-
Being slapped with the reality of what they can't
comprehend-
Trying to make amends with themselves as they
pretend-
Curling up in a ball of unreliable hope-
Treacherously searching for that endless rope-
Hoping to find something at the end of it that will
help-
Crisscrossing their paths with a fork only pointing
south-
Slowly pushing the daggers through every last part-
Finding themselves so uncontrollably mad-
So crazy, they can't be controlled, they are so very
bad-
Trying to hide themselves in someone else's
personality-
Conjuring up some kind of self-defense of their
reality-
Bursting out of their inflamed self-
Squeezing an invisible ball so they can embrace
themselves-
Wrapping their own hands around their throats-

Continuously choking themselves in some kind of
desperation to float-
Realizing they can't get rid of themselves, they are
stuck-
Using their selves as the instrument they use to
pluck-
Wearing themselves thin and complaining because
they are worn out-
They don't prevent themselves from being the ones
that is left out-
 They say, "Why I am I doing these things out of
the convenience of torturing myself"-
"Why must I do this day in and day out, I am the
one that is slowly killing myself"-

Indian Traditions

In the Old West the Indians lived in pueblos and
tepees-
These were the housing for every tribe from the
Choctaws to the Pawnees-
Some tribes when they went into battle, would paint
themselves as will as their horses-
With their bows and arrows, they would hunt for
wild game in the forest-
They had many celebrations for many events that
took place throughout the year-
They had their own myths and ways of seeking help
from the spirits-
They had medicine men and women with remedies
and herbs for healing the sick-
They would have different ceremonies for prayers
and sacrifices-
We betrayed them with our ways of civilization-
They didn't know any other way except their way
of modifications-
They had their victories and dances, such as the
ecstasy of pain-
They would make their own weapons, like
tomahawks to arrows-
 For America was once their land but was taken
away from them-
The white man came over and took it over one hand
at a time-

Where we live today is the soil that once belong to
the Native Americans-
Because of us, they had to change their ways of
living and traditions-
They didn't see things the way we did, they felt lost
in their own land-
For everything they had a different point of view-
The women did the basket weaving and the making
of clothes-
The men were the hunters, the protectors and the
bravest of men-
There are still some that live today on reservations-
And still follow the old Indian way of traditions-
To this day their beauty, habits and traditions
mystify me-
To be able to live among them two hundred years
ago would have been exciting-
For that is one race of people, who I would have
liked to have known-

Small Town

From my memories I cannot hide-
They are always there, never subside-
The way the other kids teased me in school-
But my parents said, "they are fools"-
For I was not anywhere close to being popular-
But I didn't really care if I had any friends-
But I had two friends that I truly did need then-
I hope they realize who they are, those two friends-
They didn't judge me for what I wasn't-
For they liked me for who I was-
The poor kids thought I had it so good-
They didn't understand me, I was just
misunderstood-
The middle class, they were so hung up on
themselves-
They never gave me a chance that is why I spent
most of my time to myself-
The mean girls were always trying to pick a fight
with me-
I was just glad to be away from them, they wouldn't
leave me be-
It wasn't any easier at home; the other kids just
Didn't know-
For all my pains I really never let them show-
Growing up in my small town was not my idea of
fun-

But now I would love to go back there, now that I
am not young-
I would rather live in a small town than where I live
now-
I am tired of all the building going on around me
now-
I know things by now have changed there-
Because they have surely have changed here-
Both have grown with time, such as I-
But in my heart a small town is where I feel I could
get by-
For that is where I grew up even though it was
rough-
And I am sure some of the people there, now are not
that tough-
Some kids were jealous of what I had-
I wish they could of walked one day in my shoes,
that would of have made me glad-
To help them realize what all they put me through-
So I could of teased them and made them feel sad
and blue-
But I am not that kind of person to have acted like
that-
Some of those kids should have been taught better
than that-
There was one boy that never acted that way, but I
won't mention any name-
I hope he knows who he was and I remember him
and thank him for not being that way-

Erin Schenk

The times have probably changed and those people
have grown up-
My spirits were down when I left that small town-
But someday, that is where I want to lay myself
down-
In that small town is where my family is-
But for some reason where I am now, is where my
heart is-
 Though I think about it often leaving here-
I just think to myself, "would it really be any better
off there"-
All my grandparents are gone, the places I spent
most of my time are gone-
My dad is there and my brothers and sister too-
I am here in this town now spending my time with
the man I really love-
So I think I have found where I belong-
With him, it has just taken a while to think maybe a
small town would be wrong-

Natural Balance

We wake up everyday to a world that does not
belong to us-
It belongs to someone much higher-
We are only the borrowers of this world-
We are put here to make some sense of it-
Though there are things that make no sense-
The world spins so fast that nothing last-
Time runs out for everyone and everything-
So many things changed with each existing decade-
People and things get lost along the way-
We soon led ourselves astray-
We blame someone else for something we have
done to our self-
Experimenting with things that were never meant to
be disturbed-
Causing the natural balance of life to run uneven-
We our to blame for what we have done, not God-
He is the only natural balance that exist-

Erin Schenk

Delight

Let's have a delight in everyday-
Go with delightfulness in every way-
The delightedness in a baby's smile-
It can become contagious after awhile-
When you conquer and overcome your fears-
When your heart is happy that you shed no tears-
Something that touched the inner most part of who
you are-
And every wish comes true you wished upon a star-
In a love that will last forever and just knowing
you'll never part- A moment that touches you and
mends your broken heart-
A child's heart that is innocent and pure-
When a true feeling is so right and sure-

May I Be One

That I may swim in the ocean, like a fish-
And to make use of my every wish-
To be an eagle and fly high in the sky-
Or maybe a cougar in the mountains where I am up high-
Or that fearsome grizzly bear that moves forth-
What about an owl, who hoots in the night as it, nest in a tree-
To simply be a hawk, that is bold and free-
Could I be that deer that roams in the meadow-
Maybe I am that cardinal singing outside your window-
To be that beautiful butterfly, that flies from flower to flower-
And to be that sweet smell after a long rain shower-
And maybe I am a leopard, which can move with great speed-
Just look for me, I'll be anywhere you need-
I keep an eye on you like a cat does a bird-
And I can be quiet as a mouse and not say a word-
Or to be a wild horse that grazes upon the valley-
I might be that raccoon that roams a back alley-
I could be a wild boar running through a clearing-
Or maybe the king of the jungle that every other animal fears-
I might be that elephant that move across the land and shakes the ground as I walk-

Or that puppy dog that would give anything to be
able to talk-
I could be a monkey just swinging through the
trees-
For I am the Lord, you'll never know where I will
be-

Street Living

Go ahead just walk on by, while they lay there-
As for you, you show no remorse, concern or care-
While some people who see them, look or stare-
These are the people who live among the streets-
They sometimes don't have shoes for their feet-
Searching through the trash for something to eat-
They will carry around with them everything they
have got-
And worry everyday if they will make it or not-
Most of them have lost their dignity-
And some have no more self-pity-
When you go by just think to yourself, "that could
be me"-
Then maybe you would open your eyes and see-
They just sit around with no more pride-
And just sometimes wish they would die-
But for some this is a way of life-
And they struggle just to survive-
Some drink just so they can cope-
And others have given up all hope-

Erin Schenk

Trust In Me

What is this I hear from the voice I cannot see; trust
in me-
I will do nothing to harm you, if you just trust me-
My patience will astonish you, if you just believe in
me-
I hold the bonds that will mend you together, if you
just let me-
I will dry the tears of your broken heart, if you just
love me-
I can carry your heavy burdens, if you just confide
in me-
With challenges I will help you, if you just ask me-
If you are lost and can't find your way, just find me-
I know exactly where you are, if you just look for
me-
But I am the one calling for you, so just please
answer me-

With Everyone

Lips as sweet as wine, blood like venom-
The evil at heart is dressed in denim-
Eyes that can burn right through your soul-
If touched by the hands, they will burn you hot like coal-
It is in a very desperate attempt to destroy everything-
And misery and pain it will bring-
Cutting away the inner layers of it's victim-
The lies it tells and the use of it's wisdom-
It is pounding at your door wanting to come in-
It knows how to get you, knowing exactly where to begin-
Leaving deep scars on the once unwounded heart-
Always categorizing it's next step to tear you apart-
Plotting it's evil against anyone it can take a hold of-
It will rub your soul raw, like a worn out pair of gloves-
Can you guess who it is that wants to devour all of us-
I'll give you a hint on who it is I guessed-
He is dressed in red and can disguise himself as anyone-
He can come in any form or fashion and can blend in with everyone-
He is the one who was the rejected one-
For the ones who follow him live in his darkness-

He tries to snatch us away from God's goodness-
Trying to talk people into doing what will hurt
them-
He thinks the more people he has on his side, the
more power it will give him-
He makes us do things we should have never done-
Hurting and destroying people's souls, is how he
has his fun-
For the devil can be very sneaky-
Prancing his way into someone's life that had
plenty-

Demon of Misery

I am stuck with my own demon of misery that keeps
facing me down-
Every time I think I am winning the defense, I go
back down-
In my feelings, my dreams, my pain, everywhere-
It interrupts my thoughts, pushing me over with
anything-
Draining me like a leech that could just suck out my
life-
Taking my breath and cutting every piece away
with a sharp knife-
I have to breakaway from my enemy inside me-
And open my heart to the faith that lives within me,
deep-
Be gone from me and let me breath on my own for
the first time-
Let the life I have been given be only mine-
You thought you were the one I needed for eternity-
Hoping I will cry to show my weakness-
Your misery is not going to be my darkness-
Because of you I am afraid of myself-
I have to be brave and face you down by myself-
You are going to become weak in me and empty-
I have no room for you anymore and no use for
Your pity-
I am not going to let you cause me to go numb,
Anymore-

I want to be me, not your strength of evermore-
You have me scared of who I am suppose to be-
You are slowly causing the tears to build up inside
me-
You don't care how much you hurt me, as long as
you are in control-
You make me say things I never wanted to, you
took hold-
Leave me alone; go drown in your own misery-
I don't want you to be anymore of my worry-

To Watch Over You

As the clouds slowly drift over the deep-
The waves of the ocean shuffle and sweep-
Dreaming of that shore I am laying upon-
A voice says, "there is something better far
beyond"-
I reach my hand out; I am taken by an invisible
being-
Telling me to open my eyes to what I have not been
seeing-
Like an angel, I float across the empty shore-
I am being lead, not really knowing where for sure-
A breeze moves across my face so light and gentle-
I see a vision in front of me that looks abnormal-
It is gesturing for me to come closer-
For what could it be, I wish I could see clearer-
It says to me, "I am the one that has been sent to
watch over you"-
For God knows you need me, I am something that is
true-
I am an angel that has been sent to watch over you-
I closed my eyes and think that I am dreaming-
The angel said, "I have protected you from the
start"-
For I am here where you can see me now, for you
opened up your heart-
The belief you had in me became strong- I am with
you now, where I belong-

Erin Schenk

Today the angel is still here with me as real as can
be-
And I say to God, "thank you for this angel you
have given me"-

Challenge Me

Challenge me, my heart is saying-
Come on, I want to do some playing-
I am going to beat so fast, I won't slow down-
I will race inside you until you hit the ground-
I can make you weak, I can make you strong-
When I do not beat, you will know that there is
something wrong-
I can stop you at anytime, for a minute or the rest of
your life-
It is up to you to keep me in thrive-
Because without me, you wouldn't be alive-
I am the one that has the strength to heal-
And I am the first one to know when you are ill-
If you get me to stressed out, I'll wear out-
Or do things to me you can live without-
I am what keep you going inside of you-
Because without me your life would be through-

Erin Schenk

My Quite Friend

I have this friend that is always there when I need to
talk-
She just sits quietly and listens to my thoughts-
She is in no hurry; she has got all the time in the
world-
She is right there with me no matter where I go-
She can seem to comfort me when no one else can-
She'll spend time alone with me, anytime I want-
She has no reason to judge, she knows my every
thought-
She has been with me in this life from the start-
I saw her for the first time, the first time I looked in
the mirror-
She knew there was something special about me,
showed me no fear-
To this day I still see her when I look in the mirror
and know she is near-
She is the peace that lives inside of me everyday of
every year-

Clue Not Found

Oh, how I am concerned with what passage I will
turn-
To be lost or left behind, oh, how that would make
my feelings burn-
The shattering pieces of picking myself back up,
with what strength-
Extending out my arms to reach, it is so far to
stretch the length-
Pulling myself back up out of a shallow hole-
But feeling I was anchored with a fifty-foot pole-
Looking up, but only seeing a small light, it's like I
am looking through a funnel-
These strange things run through my head like their
making a tunnel-
I try to figure out what is going on inside my head-
As I see all these pictures popping up everywhere,
the feeling of dread-
Cautiously watching the flashbacks that play
through my mind-
I look and study closely to see if there is any clue I
can find-

Erin Schenk

Scrambled Head

Go ahead and mix me up, it don't take much to
confuse-
Just overload me; I'll eventually blow a fuse-
Can't you see I am almost broken-
I am not a machine that can take many tokens-
Blind fold me and turn me around a few times, I am
lost-
You can't see where I am coming from; you have
your head buried in the frost-
Yakty, yak you just talk way to much-
No wonder you keep me confused and such-
You are more scatter brained then me-
When it happens to you, well you'll see what I
mean-
Having people laugh at you because you did
something dumb-
I bet the next time I see you; you'll be sitting in a
corner, sucking your thumb-
Scrambled up in the head just like me-
I was just sitting back and waiting to see-

We Are Loners

I'd rather have one friend than to have a whole
group-
I stayed to myself most of my youth-
I've never cared for crowds, it just isn't my thing-
I'd rather be by myself when I am doing my own
thing-
Being by myself I don't have to impress anyone
else-
Or have to worry about getting stabbed in the back
by someone else-
I use to worry about having a friend, but found one
in myself-
 There are loners everywhere that rather be by
themselves-
My husband is one, that is why we fit together so
well-
As long as we have each other, we really don't need
anyone else-
I am his companion, as well as he is mine-
We don't have to worry if the other is going to hurt
or deceive-
Our unconditional love for each other is what we
receive-
People see us together everywhere we go, we're
never apart-
That is probably made us perfect for each other
from the start-

He is my superior partner in this life, I received-
And I know he will never do anything that would
hurt me-
We were brought together to become one, how
more perfect can that be-

Tasha

Tasha, is the name of our beloved puppy dog-
She was so tiny when we got her at threes weeks
old-
She fit in the inside pocket of my husband's jacket-
Now her nose barely fits in that pocket-
She has a very unique personality-
And only takes to a few people among our family
and friends-
She has a variety of stuffed animals, I don't think
she can live without-
 Her best friend is our cat, Bobbett-
Those two are like two peas in a pod-
The way they act together sometimes is so cute, but
odd-
She is our baby, though sometimes she drives us
crazy-
Boy, sometimes she can be so lazy-
One thing she does that get on your nerves, is she
can whine-
She is a good companion and is my friend at all
times-
She sheds all the time, drives me nuts-
But she is always there for me when I feel I am in a
rut-
Or when I am upset, she tries her best to comfort me
with her love-
And as for my husband, I think she is stuck to him,
like a hand in a glove-

For she doesn't know she is one of my every things-
She has brought joy into our lives that no child
could bring-
I would not trade her for anything-

Our Love Game

In the depths of me I burn-
For, you and only you I yearn-
As fire and ice, we will melt from each other's
touch-
Passion exploding in this rush-
As you clench me in you grip-
Around my waist you tie your whip-
I feel I am bound by your rope-
When I am in your arms of endless hope-
I am buried deep beneath your caress-
You leave me tangled, I am such a mess-
As your kiss can melt me from the inside out-
When you approach me, my pleasure shouts-
Don't stop coming closer, I want you near-
I want to know your every fear-
I close my eyes and picture your next move-
You take it slow, nice and smooth-
You take your time, sending me to ecstasy-
Making sure I have my every fantasy-
I have the advantage now to make the next move-
I say lets stop playing games and make love-
Now that I am in control, what are you going to do-
I am the warrior of love now that I am in the lead-
For when I get through with you, I'll be all you
need-
The impression I leave on you, will not whelp-
You begging for mercy and there is no one to help-
Your cries are not of some enduring pain-

Erin Schenk

I'll braid you in my luscious strain-
All I want to hear is you whisper my name-
You're so good for playing our little love game-

Emptying Of The Soul

Deep down in the pits of hell lives the notorious
devil-
Always plotting new ways to do pure evil-
Bring us disaster when he rings his bell-
Wanting us to surrender to his hot, red well-
Causing people to fight against each other and kill-
He has a warped and corrupt way of getting a thrill-
Sending a evil spirit into someone and causing them
to do wrong- He has many followers to him belong-
Believe it or not, he knows how to play them all-
As they summon to their duty with each name he
calls-
Turning innocent people into immortal beast-
Causing them to rot from the evil beating in their
chest-
Lifting up his hot pitchfork and piercing a lost soul-
His game includes the emptying the goodness of a
soul-
He has a dark soul that is evil and powerful-
He rules the realms of hell and thrives on the
deceitful-
Don't let your soul be the one he empties-
Fight him off as one of your worst enemies-

Erin Schenk

One More Try

When I go to my grave I will not feel used or
borrowed-
Though many people's hearts will be filled with
sorrow-
I will be lifted up to heaven where I can hold my
head high-
I want to come back as that beautiful eagle that flies
high in the sky-
That is when I am given one more try-
Or to come back as a mighty warrior that conquers
the world- Maybe to be what I always wanted to be
and much more-
 Or maybe as Amazon Princess from a time long
ago-
To be a vigorous captain of an old battleship that
sailed the seas to and fro-
That is if I was given one more try-
To be so wondrous I could fix everything that was
wrong-
To come back as someone who is mighty and
strong-
To live out every dream the best that I can-
And be bold enough to take in everything I can
withstand-
Just to prove it all to myself with one more try-
Not to be the burden carrier I was once upon a time-
But to be a Queen and ruler that is the most kind-

To make things less complicated for the people who
don't understand-
To be given the time to give everything one more
try-
To come back as an angel to someone that needs
one the most-
And never to be a haunting and evil ghost-
To be a spirit that will live on that protects the
helpless-
To have a chance to be everything all over again-
To love everything from beginning to end-
For one more try is all I need to satisfy me-

Erin Schenk

Sorted Out

I lie awake unable to sleep from the fast moving
traffic in my head-
The different pictures of things I need to do, but so
far never did-
Tangled collaborations run through hitting each
other, bang, boom-
There is that room in my head that needs to be
cleaned and vacuumed-
It is damp and musky and truly needs to be aired
out-
Everything is just crammed together; nothing is
sorted out-

Permission To Speak

I know I am young and I shouldn't put my two
cents in-
I am told to be quiet and just listen-
Don't speak unless spoken to-
I have been told to interrupt, is rude the thing to do-
And if you listen you'll learn more-
I get in trouble for speaking out of turn-
For my parents are always trying to teach me
manners, I guess this is one-
I was told it rude to cut someone off when they're
in the middle of saying something-
My parents are right; I don't like being cut off when
I am saying something-
So I am just asking for permission to speak-

Been Set

For many times I have cried-
Close to the beginning of life, I died twice-
Struggling with many different trials-
And felt I was walking down a road of endless
miles-
Coming to a crossroad with a hundred different
directions-
Receiving nothing, but meaningless connections-
Drowning in my sorrow for things I couldn't
change-
Bringing about things that made me feel deranged-
And this inclination for an embroidered meaning-
The spell my mind cast upon my heart and my sense
of feeling-
And the emptiness that lies in the pit of my
stomach-
To banish the thoughts that make my head ache-
Looking for a memory in my uncategorized files-
Not sure of what I am looking for as I sift through
the piles-
Needing to organize my priorities so bad-
But everything I try to figure out where to start, I
get frustrated and mad-
I just want to through everything up in the air and
say, "forget it"-
And sometimes I feel I am in a smaller body than a
cricket-

But then I think, "why am I getting myself so
upset"-
For everything that happens has already been set-

Daydreaming of Sandy Shores

As you lie there upon the shores and the waves
come crashing in-
The relaxation of that moment as your body goes
limp-
The water is so soothing; you feel you could melt
with it-
Peace and serenity surround you, as there is no
hectic noise, just nature-
You need this to feel at peace with yourself and
nurtured-
You breathe in the fresh air and soak up all of this
you can-
The birds are flying, the wind is blowing and your
feet feel good in the sand-
Your mind is at ease, you have no stress-
You just leave everything behind that was such a
mess-
Than you realize you are sitting at your desk at a
busy office-
Your phone is ringing off the hook and you realize
you were just daydreaming, that was obvious-

Time Slipped Through My Hands

The glass slipped from my hand and shattered on
the floor-
I started picking up the pieces, cut my finger, but
something inside of me hurt much deeper-
As I continued to pick up the pieces I felt I was
Picking up pieces of my life-
For the broken pieces of glass were sharper than a
knife-
At that moment I realized how much I let slip
through my hands-
The memories I could have saved if only a little
strand-
All the times I forgot to say "I love you" to who
mattered most-
And not tied all my painful feelings to a wooden
post-
To have spent more time with my grandparents,
when they were here-
The time I spent growing up and not seeing every
obstacle-
Time goes by so fast that is seems like it's never
going to stop-
I push myself so hard at times just to reach the top-
Why do I do this when so much time maybe left-
I guess that so much time has gone by wasted that I
am just trying to get all I can-

Devouring Beast

Lurking behind the shadows is a devastating beast-
The only time it comes out and moves about is at
night-
It is hideous and disgusting and feeds on the flesh-
Looking for any kind of morsel that is warm
and fresh-
Satisfying it's hunger with anything it can-
It will devour every ounce of meat-
Hiding and watching it's next victim-
Its spit is poison, like venom-
It will chase its meal until it is wore it out-
The poor thing has no strength left, it just
bellows and shouts-
It is so fast that nothing knows it is coming-
And so quiet nothing knows it is moving-
It is always on the prowl for some helpless prey-
For its teeth are so sharp and never will decay-
The deep still of the night is when it goes hunting-
It flies to where it wants to go, while searching-
His dungeon is full of many skeletons-

Hidden Beauty

The veil across her face hides her beauty-
Her nakedness is forbidden to be seen-
Her hair is placed atop her head under a scarf-
The jewels that hang around her neck, accent her
breast-
Her slender design is for only one man to touch-
He is the one and only that is allowed to see it all-
Her love for him is his and no one else's-
Their desire for each other is theirs alone-
Her eyes say so much, though she hardly speaks-
Her body is his temple which he dwells upon-
When they touch, they go to another world-
A world full of passion and desire and of course
love-
He knows her every part and knows how to turn her
on-
She knows every inch of his body, is hers alone-
Cradled in his arms she is safe-
Their bed is never cold or full anger-
As they both lay together warm and tender-
Her face fits perfectly into his hands-
While her caress and tender touch is all he needs-
He knows her unique love is very rare-
She is his hidden beauty he will hold forever-

Erin Schenk

Life Is A Gamble

Life is a gamble that cheats you-
Sometimes misdirects you in the wrong direction-
Pain and suffering comes from living, life-
Some things are taken away, some things are given-
It is a game that everyone has learned to play-
Life can be so cruel, just when you think everything
is going to be alright-
It causes you to some times give up and other times
to fight-
God gave us all our own lives to test us, to see how
we would handle it-
He makes every determination before we can make
it-
He turned everyone of us lose to see if we would
make something of it or not-
He brings the real things to our lives that we can't
control-
For He rolls the dice to determine our next move-
It can be to slow us down, speed us up or make us
come to a complete stop-
Life is a serious game to take and play seriously-
Never make the wrong move to cheat yourself or
someone else and play it carefully-
We are in this life game until we win or lose-
For God knows which ones at the right time to
choose-

Cramped Room

At the end of this hallway there is this most
particular room-
In this room there are many unusual things-
For each time you open the door, there is something
different to see-
From people dancing at a party to monkeys
swinging through the trees-
Just open your imagination and this room will take
you anywhere you want to go-
You can go places where no one else has to know-
Something different for any kind of mood-
Like slumber parties to going to the zoo-
Open your imagination and just walk into this
room-
You'll see all kinds of things from royal balls to
dancing brooms-
So visit this room and see where it takes you-

Brave Little Knight

In his room are pictures of great knights-
He thinks they were so brave to go into battle and
fight-
He has his plastic sword and his shiny armor-
He tries to be so brave and fight off fire breathing
dragons-
He pretends to ride his noble steed through the
woods and beyond-
He'll trample upon anything that gets in his way-
He thinks he is so mighty and sure, that is how he
wants to stay-
Fighting off the bad to preserve the good-
He knows he can drive all the evil away, he knows
he could-
He dreams so much of being a king's royal knight-
He tells his parents in his past life he was a brave
knight-

Delicate Jewel

Lying beneath his caress with her nakedness-
Waiting one again for him to leave her breathless-
He aggressively throws back the covers-
She tell him, "if you're not a good boy I won't be
your lover"-
As he starts at her feet and his hands move up her
body of expectations-
He proceeds to touch her every part with extreme
caution-
He handles her delicately, as if she is priceless
jewel-
As for what they do to each other, there is no rules-
She is rare and sweet; he must handle her with care-
For he is her priceless jewel and with no one will
she share-
His heart belongs to her; she is the only one that
holds the key-
As she lies there and feels his every touch, every
kiss, she is all he sees-
His body forms to hers and becomes one shadow-
He knows he has the most prizes possession, her
delicate love-

Lost Love

This lost love was so very special, no one could fill
the void-
The love they shared was so very different from any
other-
They understood each other like no one else could-
The other knew exactly what the other one needed-
At one time they were inseparable, never apart-
How it was missed, everything about them-
The smell, the touch, the kiss, the feelings, the love,
everything-
There is not a day that goes by that person is not in
their thoughts-
 Nothing or no one can contain this emptiness they
feel-
Though it has been many years, they have not
forgotten one thing-
Remembering them down to every little detail-
There is a place in their heart that person will stay
forever-

Soul To You

Just love me and I will touch your heart-
Wrap yourself up in me and I will keep you from
the cold-
Be my soul mate for a lifetime to come-
One touch of my hand, you will realize there is no
need to run-
The music in my heart will play in you-
Forever I will be tied and bound to your soul, to
you-
I give you every part of me to love and hold-
My breath is your breath, my heart is your heart,
and I share it all with you-
The kisses I give you are meant for you and only
you-
My arms were meant to hold you and my love for
you was meant to be given-
We were soul mates once upon a time, maybe in
heaven-
Again we have been brought together for some
purpose-
I want to be deep within you, your love I want to
poses-
Love, make passionate love until we can't go on-
Lighthearted and free we will be, the feelings will
never be wrong-
Slowly this accentuating power of lust, passion, and
desire takes over-

We can't hide from it, for there is no need for shelter
or cover-
The lavishing feeling of uncontrolled desire takes
possession-
Our souls feel like they are being lifted into
unbelievable passion-
My body aches and yearns to become one with
yours-
We have no need to rush, to resolve this matter may
take hours-
I am your mate and you are mine-
For the love I have for you is very strong and a
straight line-
Believing in this special bond we share makes our
love true-
For every moment I love you, my soul will have a
place for you-

Love of Dance

The beat of those drums pound in her heart as she
dances-
And everyone else dances as well by the campfire
light-
The music is blazing in her soul and carries her-
In her eyes and her body, you can see the passion
for her love of dance-
She knows how to move with the beat of the drums-
She is completely under the spell of the music-
Her body sways without any thought-
Her mind is captivated by the sound of the flutes-
Her tan, red skin glistens as the fire shines on her-
Her long black hair flows around her face as she
moves-
The men watch her in astonishment and see her
passion for dance-
The women want to feel as free as she does-
Her shadow makes the same movements she makes-
Her love of dance she will never let fade-

Erin Schenk

Out Of This Town

I want out of this town, I don't want to be here-
I want to be away from the traffic and people; I
want quietness near-
Here I feel like I am being smothered, no where to
run-
I want to be in the woods again, that sounds like
fun-
To be alone with no one around, run naked if I dare-
Go to my special hideout and if the world fell apart,
I would not care-
As long as I had everything I needed at the place I
want to go-
Where I am now, is to busy for me, I want out-
To be able to sit on my porch wrapped up only in a
blanket if I want-
To be in the country where the whippoorwills sing-
And to sit on my porch swing and only hear the
natural things-
I hate it here; I want to be closer to God so He can
hear-
Because of all the noise here, I don't think He hears
me clear-
I don't know if many people understand where I am
coming from-
This is not where I want to spend the rest of my life,
I want to run-

Red Velvet Curtain

Behind the red velvet curtain was this door that
would lead you to anywhere you wanted to go-
To a land of dinosaurs or to a magical fairyland-
Or a beautiful castle where the most loyal King and
Queen lived-
To a valley with rivers and streams with a log cabin
with smoke coming out of the chimney-
Maybe a mountain you would like to climb and
conquer-
There could be a land where pioneers lived and
settled-
Or maybe a village where the people only know
how to love and care for each other-
Maybe just a bench with that person sitting there,
you are suppose to spend the rest of your life with-

United Nation

The Indians were robbed of their land-
We, took it away from them just by one hand-
This was once the soil of the Native Americans-
Where they hunted for buffalo and wild game-
They had their sacred medicines of healing-
Their sacred healing dances for the sick-
The great spirit of their hearts as they became one
tribe-
The legends of each tribe was so astonishing-
If I could of lived two hundred years ago among
these people-
I would have learned the true value of life-
I read about them and dream of what it would have
been like-
To live among the Indians and learned from them-
To be part of their rituals and sacred events-
Being close to one another as they united as one-
Being a part of something that went down in
history-
Never knowing the ways of the world, as it is today-
They were once a very strong and united nation-
Not knowing that one day it would be swept away-

Fall of Mankind

The fall of mankind, we are doing with our own
hands-
No one realizes we are doing this to ourselves, some
will never understand-
The ways we wage war on one another is our
biggest fall-
Before we know it, we will destroyed us all-
We will merely be a memory like the things that
have become extinct-
There will be a time we will all go crazy and not be
able to think-
We will all start killing each other off because we
won't know any better-
We are slowly coming to our end, which is going to
be bitter-
The tragedies we face today will seem so simple to
the one's we will have to face-
We will not be able to run from each other, there
will be no safe place-
God will send His wrath down on us, hard-
He has given us plenty of warning for us to put up
our guard-
But we have refused to listen to His instructions-
He is going to be mankind's destruction-
 He has given us plenty of time to change our ways
and has a lot patience-

Erin Schenk

We ignored His message a hundred times over; He
is growing, impatient-
Some haven't learned the importance of what He is
been trying to teach us-
Some look at God as an enemy and look at Him in
disgust-
Blaming Him for the way their lives turned out-
Never thinking it was their own fault of the turn of
events that came about-
Mankind has had so many chances to do things
right-
We continue to do things wrong, for the wrong
reasons and fight-

Memories Of My Daddy

Riding upon my daddy's shoulders, as we would
walk through the woods-
I felt so safe, secure and tall, I knew he would
protect me, he always would-
He would tickle me until I couldn't breath and I
laughed so hard-
When he would come home on the weekends, he'd
Work in the yard-
He traveled to different countries from Portugal to
Israel-
Sending me home dolls from all over the world-
During the winter was hunting season and he would
never miss a season-
He always did what he would say, never come up
with another reason-
When I was little, he seemed so tall-
For when I was a baby in his arms, I probably
seemed so small-
He made sure I had all the comforts I needed-
And going to have breakfast with him at his favorite
restaurant on Saturday mornings-
Just being with him when he was home had so
much meaning-
He is still alive today, but lives in my heart, always-
While the love I will always have for my daddy will
never delay-

Erin Schenk

The One

I saw you standing there waiting in the light of the
moon-
You knew I was coming to meet you soon-
I ran to you from across the shore-
You showed me a love I never saw before-
In our embracement I felt this immediate spark-
In your eyes there was this satiable light I could see
it in the dark-
For you, I felt this most incredible sensation of lust-
You had to be mine, you just must-
The fiery storms of my thoughts were focused on
you-
I knew you were the one to make all my dreams
come true-

Don't Judge Me

Do not judge me for who I have become-
Judgment against me from you is not welcome-
You don't know me, so how do you know how I
am-
For I should not be the one with the name that gets
smudged-
You don't know what lies in the depths of my heart-
For what lies inside maybe the truth-
You have no authority to judge anyone but yourself-
Understand you have to see what is in you before
you can talk about me-
I can be your friend or your worst enemy-
Please leave the job to God to judge any of us-
He is the only one that knows the real truth that
should be judged-

Choose Your Life

Make a good decision that is right for your life-
Don't sell yourself short, cutting your own throat,
with this life- Fight for what you want out of this
life-
Choose the right path to carry you along your
journey-
But don't rush anything, take your time, don't
worry-
You have the choice to make your life what you
want-
Don't hold anything back, get out there and flaunt-
Think carefully of what you want most-
And for goodness sakes don't be someone else's
ghost-
For every opportunity is possible for you-
But it is up to you to choose the life that is right for
you-

Legion Of The Strong

Dreaming of being alone in my own land-
Only compromising what I want from what
surrounds me-
Not answer to any other authority, but my own-
But maybe to live among a people as equal as I-
To have no ruler and only have peace living in our
hearts-
To be one little unity under one sky-
A beautiful and peaceful place that is surrounded by
love-
Never looking for a way to hurt anyone-
To be bonded together by a sacred grace-
And to be a legion of unbelievable love and
strength-
To hold each other's hands and remain strong-
Our strength will come together as one-
We will conquer anything or anyone that looks to
harm us-
We will stand and fight together to protect our love
and hope-
One will not survive without the other to keep us
remaining strong-
We will never let go of either one without a fight-
We are proud of our belief and honor these two-
Our greatest hope lives in our souls-
Our greatest love lives in our hearts-
In our legion one cannot function without the other-

Erin Schenk

We will remain strong if we hold love and hope
close to us-
There will never be pain or sorrow among us in our
village-
We will not grow old in our hearts, knowing our
legacy must go on-

Follow My Own

The demons in my head are mine alone-
They cause corruption that is my own-
Causing me at times not to be me-
Coming out of the crevasses where they cut me
deep-
Making me believe the bad side of my soul, is right-
They feel like they are trying to suck the good out
of my every might-
My every might that I may use to fight them off-
Sometimes I feel they have all the power over my
every emotion-
I know I must remain strong to fight off their true
notion-
They make me want to do things that would be my
destruction-
They want me to follow them to their destination-
No thank you, I will follow my own-
For you demons, you are not where I want my heart
to make itself at home-
I won't let you have the power over me like you
would another-
My will is to fight you off and love God like there is
no other-
They try to drown me when they see me swimming
my way to the top-
 They don't want me to reach where I need to be,
they want me to stop-
The darkness is where they dwell-

Erin Schenk

That is where they want me as well-
I know the good in my heart, is my true calling-
I will not let them be the ones that cause my falling-

Open My Eyes

I need to see where I am going, to see what I can
reach-
Holding on to what is seen when I open my eyes-
Looking into a soul of someone and seeing their
beauty-
Seeing things that I have seen before, but seeing
them for the first time-
Using my eyes to learn more about the things I see-
To look for beauty in something that was once ugly
to me-
No matter who or what it is I see, look at them with
more grace-
Being more focused on the good of what I see,
instead of the bad- Not judging by what I see on the
outside, but taking a look on the inside-
I may see the ugliness in something that I thought
was beautiful before-
To see the beauty that God put into everything that
He made-
To look deep into the eyes of someone I love and
find myself there-
Also to look deep inside me and find that special
beauty that is in me-
I am opening my eyes for the first time after all
these years-
I wonder why I didn't before, because there is
beauty somewhere out there-

Erin Schenk

Young Lovers

Hearts of fire burn strong in two young lovers-
They run wild with each other under the covers-
Neither one has ever felt this kind of feeling before-
They are equal in the satisfaction they get from each
other-
People say they're too young to understand what
they are doing-
They both know exactly what they want, each
other's love, and forever-
For they are in tranquility of one another's embrace-
Their love for each other will stand the test of time,
forever-
They have promised each other to spend eternity
together-
Never going astray to look or seek any other-
They will runaway if they have to, just so no one
will break them apart-
She carries something that belongs to the both of
them-
For he has broken the seed that has put new life into
her-
That makes their love even stronger-
She is all he ever wanted and so much more-
He holds the sacred key to her heart-
From her, he never wants to part-
Their families will not keep them apart-

They have realized they are each other's forever
heart-

Wrong For Me

The evil in this world is wrong for me, I wasn't
designed that way-
To follow a crowd that destroys the things that are
precious-
My goodness is all mine, I have the choice to share-
When I do things terribly wrong, part of me feels
destroyed-
I ask for forgiveness, hoping that will save me-
I know, me talking about people is wrong, but
sometimes I can't help it-
Sometimes, some things make me want to be bad, it
is hard to control-
Some how I will get punished for being a bad girl-
Like raising my voice and saying things I never
meant to say-
Saying very wrong things to someone I love the
most and hurting them-
Slandering and cussing myself for screwing up, at
the same time knowing better-
Feeling bad for treating myself wrong- Instead of
quieting myself, I keep screwing with myself-
Everything won't get better if I don't stop all of
this-
I create problems for myself when I don't let things
go-
The trash that other people has collected in my
mind is wrong for me-

There has to be a clean path for me; that is just right
for me-

I Can't, Without You

I can't help the way you make me feel-
It feels so wonderful, right and real-
The thrills I get just being close to you-
I can't believe you, are so true-
I hope I never have to make it without you-
I can't imagine the way that would feel, without
you-
We are everything to one another-
You are my heart, my husband, my friend and my
lover-
I will never be sorry you are a part of me-
I can't, without you, be all I ever wanted to be-
I can't thank you enough for loving all of me-
Without you in my life I probably would not be this
happy-
I can't imagine my life without you; I love you-
Without you I wouldn't have become what I am
today-
I can't believe you were the one given to me-
Without you I wouldn't have learned all I needed
to-
Without you I wouldn't be where I am today-
You were sent to me to show me, I can-
And I was sent to show you, someone will love you
all they can-

They Don't Understand

They don't understand all I can be-
They really don't know the real me-
I am not that little girl they once knew-
I am a woman now with my own point of view-
I have my own mind made up of the right thing to
do-
I grew up scared, wondering of what I would
become-
For I knew I had it in me to be someone, who was
not dumb-
The determination of what I had in me, even
amazed me-
I didn't know I had all these special gifts of who I
could be-
They never really paid attention at what was inside-
Only looking at me from the outside-
The smartness and sharpness I have learned about
myself-
I found so many different wonderful things inside
me without anyone's help-
May my book change my family's point of view
about me-
To bring us closer some how, like we should be-

Erin Schenk

Timid Spirits

Timid spirits float about scared and lost-
Scarred from the pain that won't set them free-
They try to grasp for some kind of release-
Attempting in any desperation to not feel wounded-
Bound by some kind of injustice that just won't let
them go-
For they are trapped in between worlds they don't
know-
Wondering where they have ended up, never sure-
Desperately searching for an answer of where they
are suppose to be-
They jump at any sudden movement, afraid of being
attacked-
Not sure of what is coming up from behind, they
can't look back-
Broken into a million pieces that can't be put back
Together-

All Right, I Surrender

I surrender myself to you; you've got me-
My battlement with you is over, you have won my
heart-
My defenses are down; I am not a mighty warrior
when you are near-
You can take me as your prisoner; I promise I will
cooperate-
But when I am away from you I have unbelievable
strength-
You make me weak in ways I never felt before-
My love surrenders to you every time we are
together-
No matter what I do, I cannot fight it-
I never surrender to anyone, but you-
You have got me exactly where you want me-
Do what you want with me, do as you please-
Astonish me with everything you have got-
My sword, my body, my strength, my heart,
everything surrenders to you-
The passion I feel for you is stronger than any
passion I have ever felt for anything or anyone else-
Will you surrender to me if I ask you to-
For the weakness in you hungers for me-
You may be the mightiest of all the men, but that
won't help-
Your battlement with me has just started-
And in the end we will both win-

Erin Schenk

So I am surrendering to you everything that is warm
and tender-
A side of me that no one has ever seen before-
I am the woman that is equal to your strength-
For I can go for however long you can-
It won't take long for you to know, I surrender-
The sword I carry is my strength, but you are my
weakness-
No other man can cause the rapture you do-
That is why I will always surrender to you-

Honor My Heart; Hold My hand

I acknowledge the things in my heart, though
sometimes I don't understand-
All I want is for someone to be there, to hold my
hand-
And honor the feelings in my heart that will
sometimes cause me to break-
 My hand is reaching out for someone, for someone
to take-
 The strength in the hand I hold must be strong-
And the honor in their heart must promise to never
do me wrong-
To understand that there are things I can't
comprehend-
Help me get through my struggles and just hold my
hand-
My heart knows what is best for me, it knows I can-
And the honor that is in my heart, I will always hold
in my hands-

Still Not Rescued

I am unsure of where I am going and not clear on
where I have been-
I feel like I have been lost my whole life-
Just waiting for someone to rescue me, but who-
The things I have tossed at myself to try to get
through-
I was burying myself deeper in my mixed up
emotions-
Simply looking for an answer that was never there-
I would slide myself down an endless waterfall and
never reaching the bottom-
Trapped in my own misery, the way I had become-
I would listen to the voices in my head that was
confused-
Ignoring what my heart was trying to say-
Letting myself get so far down, I felt there was no
way up-
Still begging for someone to rescue me-
I would lie and wait, but no one would come-
Laying in the pits on my own destruction-
Causing myself mental anguish from everything I
felt-
Never asking for the real answer of how I could
rescue me-
All I had to do was ask for help from up above-
I can't believe it took me so long to reach out-
I still wouldn't have been rescued if it weren't for
His help-

To Touch Her Once

As he closes his eyes and sees her in his mind-
Because every time he wants to say something to
her, he backs away-
He is scared to say the wrong thing and scare her
Away-
She is the most beautiful woman he has ever seen
before-
From her long dark hair to her long slender legs and
everything in between-
He gets turned on by her, every time she gets close-
But she doesn't know he feels this way about her-
He has been in love with her from the first time he
saw her-
She doesn't even know he is there, but he is always
near-
He wishes he could touch her just once-
For he knows she is the most rare thing he has ever
came close to-
He hides his feelings from her even though he sees
her everyday-
He knows she lives alone, because he is the ghost in
her home-
They were together in a time from long, long ago-
So in love, but he was taken away from her, because
the angers of war-
They were suppose to marry, but never got to make
it that far-
His spirit is lonely for hers; still after all this time-

But her spirit has not met up again with his in this
lifetime-
All he wants and all he'll ever want, is just to touch
her once again-

Out Of The Darkness

I was lead out of the darkness by a warm and kind
hand-
I had hid myself in a far, dark and painful land-
Some how I conceived the brightness that was
always there for me-
My eyes were opened to wonderful things that I was
just waiting to see-
My blindness was gone, even though I could see
before-
This brightness had a love I never felt and much
more-
The darkness I walked in was lonely and cold-
I knew I wanted out of it before I grew old-
I use to have the feelings I would never be able to
come out-
My eyes filled with tears when I felt I was being
lead out-
I had a lightness, in my heart that I never felt
before, it felt incredible-
It made me feel everything was possible-
I wondered if I would ever walk out of the
darkness-
Until one day I was shown that I could walk right
into the my own brightness-
It was like my fears were lifted and taken far away-
I made my brightness all possible by just reaching
out to pray-

Erin Schenk

Learning To Survive

One can be sheltered to much and not learn what
life is all about-
While another is set lose to learn for themselves
what it's all about-
Some are never taught to survive when disaster
strikes-
Always handed everything on a silver platter-
There are other's who are taught that surviving is
the only way to live-
But it is sad when there is some that have never
known the difference-
Never knowing how to take care of themselves
when something does go wrong-
And when the world comes to an end like it has
been written, no one will survive-
Nothing will exist, except for some lost memories-
In the meantime between now and then, we all must
learn to survive-
No matter what we have or don't have, we must
appreciate what we do have-
It can all be taken away from us so fast, we are left
with nothing-
Some people think they can buy anything and
everything they need-
But they don't realize there are things out there they
need more, they can never buy-

When tragedy happens, it takes great strength to
Survive-
Things can happen to anyone at anytime, there is no
way to see it coming-
For things are thrown at us that can be so severe-
Just hold on to faith and strength to hold you
together-

Angel of Grace

I hold in my heart the things I can't hold in my
hand-
So many memories, they are endless like grains of
sand-
I am like a tree with many branches still in tact-
I have held many people with no need to attack-
I have helped them to arrive to their destination in
safety-
My mission is to raise them up to the heavenly-
To give grace and peace to people when they lose
someone-
To keep a watchful eye on the ones that will arrive
at His Kingdom-
I lead them to a place that is not filled with pain and
sorrow-
I am there to help when disaster strikes and the
things that follow-
I heal hearts and souls that have been broken-
For everything I do to help is with God's special
token-
My job is very difficult when there is so much to
take in-
I know when I arrive; the healing I send must begin-
It may take some people along time to get over with
what comes about-

I can hear everything from someone's whimper to
their loudest shout-
God sends me to try my best to make everything
Alright-
And if my job is watch over someone, I will do it
with all my might-
For I am one of the many special angels that live in
heaven-

Erin Schenk

Amazing Light

This amazing light comes out of nowhere-
With the brilliance of peace so near-
Showing me my path that I must walk-
I am in such shock, I can barely talk-
A voice speaks to me and introduces itself-
I think to myself, "it is God, Himself"-
It says, "walk with me, I have much to share"-
"I have many thing s to show you, don't be scared"-
The infinite path I am sending you down will have
many answers-
For you have waited for answers to your prayers-
Many times you asked for things to change in your
life-
You are right on track with a few brief delays-
For you have your role to play, while others have
their roles to play-
Once you realize your purpose in this life, is your
path that is true-
For every thought you have, I have already seen-
No matter what you have done, I know where you
have been-
I have given you many mistakes for you to correct-
In hoping you would grow and mature with life and
connect-

With what the meaning of your life is all about-
To compose your own beauty from the interior and
let it come out-
I built you and put into you exactly what I wanted-
I knew you would be special for the mission I was
sending you on-
Your life was a hard struggle at first, but I was
preparing you to be strong-
I sent you down many paths testing you, so you
could see where you belong-
You battled many demons that continuously caused
you to do wrong-
With my help I know the path of light, I have shown
you is right-
I will walk with you and hold your hand tight-

Epilogue

I was scared of where my life was headed when I was growing up. I wasn't sure of what I would become and not sure if I had any special gifts I could share with others. Now that I am grown up, it took me awhile to realize the gifts I did receive. The thoughts, the feelings and meanings I put into my writing, I have learned a lot about myself in a very short period of time. Things I learned about myself that has always been there. I always dreamed of writing a book, but never thought it would happen. Now I have, and I have never been more proud of myself. The things I have written in this book have changed my life so much. I have my husband to thank, because every time I wanted to give up, he wouldn't let me.
But God had the biggest hand in it, and I thank Him so very much.

Love And Peace, From My Heart

Erin Schenk

Printed in the United States
68618LVS00001B/1-39

9 780978 763114